BROKEN TO BETTER

BROKEN

TO

BETTER

13 Ways Not to Fail at
Life and Leadership

MICHAEL KURLAND

HOUNDSTOOTH
PRESS

BROKEN TO BETTER

13 Ways Not to Fail at Life and Leadership

FIRST EDITION

ISBN   978-1-5445-2972-1 *Hardcover*

      978-1-5445-2970-7 *Paperback*

      978-1-5445-2971-4 *Ebook*

To Alejandra, my amazing wife, you help me to Be Better every day. To my future son or daughter. I love you already.

CONTENTS

INTRODUCTION

Be Better.

Coming out of a divorce and dealing with a job that did nothing for me other than provide a paycheck, I knew I wanted my life to be better. The question keeping me awake at night was "Is this all there is?" I had hit rock bottom personally and professionally.

As a child of an alcoholic father, I entered my twenties and thirties already broken. I thought I had done all the right things: college degree, good job, marriage. In reality, I was clueless about what it meant to be better, but I knew I had to make major changes.

My initial focus was on my physical health. I committed to healthier eating and regular exercise. I began meditating and journaling to strengthen my body, mind, and spirit. As my physical and mental health improved, I focused on my career and realized I wanted to launch a business with the concept of "being better" rooted throughout the entire organization. The success of this strategy led me to write this book.

I'm confident that, like me, you're looking for something better for yourself and your business. Being a business owner is not for the faint of heart. At a minimum, it takes a person with a firm resolve, the ability to persevere and pivot during challenging times, the humility to admit mistakes, and empathy for the people around them. Self-reflection should come long before setting pen to paper for a business plan. Understanding who you are is critical to being a leader who seeks to align purpose with profit.

When I set out cross-country from New York to California to launch Branded Group, Be Better became my singular purpose. I realized that, as a CEO, I must lead by example so that my team would also be motivated and inspired to do the same.

This simple phrase has been the bedrock of my company culture, driving us to go above and beyond for our clients, our colleagues, our community, and each other. It is the beacon that guides our daily business decisions and sets the course for our long-term strategy.

In addition to wanting to lead a successful business, I wanted my company to be generous and actively involved in the community. My employees needed to embrace a "socially responsible" mindset so that our collective motivation was generosity of our time, talent, and resources. My role as a CEO is to leave a legacy that has a positive impact on others, whether it's because we provided meals to the food insecure, helped build sustainable housing for those most in need, or provided tuition assistance for a future tradesperson.

Broken to Better is for business leaders who are seeking to Be Better in their company, for their employees, clients, and community. Over the course of writing this book, my team and I have experienced a global pandemic, quarantines, and what seemed like never-ending wildfires in our beautiful state of California. None of us had previously experienced these types of challenges, and our agility muscles have been stretched to the max. However, we continue to be firmly focused on our vision, purpose, and core values, which has enabled us to persevere through what seemed impossible.

Putting time and effort into your company's culture is an investment that will reap rewards for years. Creating a work environment that is welcoming, nurturing, and empowering will keep your team engaged and ready to service your clients with excellence. As you get to know your team—*really* know them—you will begin to break down the old hierarchies created around the idea of "I'm the CEO, and you're not." Of course, you are the CEO. You make all the big decisions. But at the end of the day, you are a person just as the people who work for you are also people. If you can level the playing field in their eyes so that they feel comfortable talking to you as a person, not just as a boss they're fearful of, you've created a culture of gratitude, empathy, and compassion.

During my tenure as CEO of Branded Group, I've been able to speak at industry conferences and write articles that have been published in trade magazines and digital publications. I have even launched my own podcast sharing the Be Better stories of other entrepreneurs, CEOs, and business leaders. It's been an amazing journey and one I look forward to continuing for years to come.

I have learned many lessons during the course of my entrepreneurial journey. These have come from my co-founders, my employees, and our clients and vendors, as well as a multitude of industry experts I have had the privilege to meet and interact with regularly. You will read about many of these lessons and the various teachers I've had in this book. I'm happy to share their insights so that you, my fellow entrepreneur, can take advantage of the experiences I've had and perhaps avoid some of the missteps.

This book consists of 13 principles that will inform and inspire you to Be Better in all aspects of your life—to be a better CEO, manager, employee, friend, coworker, or whatever shoes you fill. Some of the tips and best practices may seem like common sense. You may be tempted to gloss over them, but I recommend that you take it all in, as there's always something new to learn. I also hope you will check out the podcast recommendations at the end of each chapter. The guests on these shows are both informative and inspiring.

If you walk away from reading this book with only one lesson, it is to lead with emotional intelligence. Making money is a good thing, and I hope you will see how my team and I have been able to create and sustain a profitable company. However, I believe our success was achieved because of our Be Better commitment and our company culture.

This book reflects my personal experience of being an entrepreneur. Yours is likely to look different, as it should. Yet I hope the topics and examples I share will help you navigate the ups and downs of business ownership. Whether you are a solopreneur or a leader of a multinational corporation, it is my desire that you will gain a new perspective on what it means to be a purpose-driven leader in the 21st century.

If each of us committed to the Be Better mantra and approached each day with gratitude, imagine the world we'd be able to create for future generations! I challenge you to figure out your own way to Be Better so that your imprint on this planet will endure.

I don't know what challenges, personal or professional, will be in front of you as you read this book. But if, as CEOs and business leaders, we continue to be humble, to lead with integrity, and to Be Better, there's nothing we can't accomplish.

I wish you the best in life and leadership!

CHAPTER 1

BE CONNECTED

Starting with Who You Know

When I graduated college with my degree in sports management, I thought a career in the industry would easily follow. I presumed I'd start in an entry-level position and work my way up into management. Before long, I'd be living the dream with a career in baseball.

Then 9/11 happened and completely upended this plan. I had to quickly pivot to find a job. My first step was to reach out to the brothers in my fraternity, Phi Delta Theta. Surely someone would be hiring.

We've all heard the saying, "It's not what you know; it's who you know." Unless you're a young kid, it's likely you know hundreds, if not thousands, of people. Be connected. Each of them has or will have something to offer at some point in your journey.

Because of my connections, I landed an interview with the Carolina Panthers. While I didn't get the job, the interview experience itself was an exciting opportunity. My first real job was a stint as a substitute teacher. Knowing teaching was not my calling, I tapped into my fraternity brotherhood once again and secured a job as a store manager in training at a large clothing retailer. Later, I used my network to seek out my next role. An entry-level position for a facility manager was available at a large apparel company, where my friend's father was the executive vice president of real estate. Not knowing what a facility manager was, but realizing I had to pay my bills, I took the job.

These humble beginnings are what expanded my professional network and strengthened my sales and relationship-building skills. They were truly "fake it until you make it" gigs, and I would not have had these opportunities without my fraternity membership. I still reach out to this group regularly. During the COVID-19 pandemic, we checked in with each other often. It's one of the strongest networks I have.

To launch and grow a business, you're going to need help—*a lot* of help. If you think you can do it on your own, you will quickly learn that is a recipe for feeling frustrated and overwhelmed. You will burn out, and the motivation to strike out on your own will disappear faster than your bank account balance.

Even if you plan to be a solopreneur, you need to have an internal "board of directors" that includes, at minimum, a lawyer, a banker, an accountant, and a trusted friend or colleague. These advisors can help you get through the myriad of tasks that will get your business off the ground and help it grow through its various stages. Let's face it: we don't know everything, and relying on experts from time to time may prevent a lot of sleepless nights.

The following are some practical tips on how to Be Connected and expand your network.

SHOW UP WELL

My first tip is simple: show up well. What do I mean by this? Despite what you may have heard, first impressions are lasting. People rarely forget them.

Therefore, when attending an event or meeting, dress the part. In fact, don't be afraid to "peacock it" a little to ensure you stand out. It sounds elementary, but I've been to hundreds of events, and I'm always surprised at the casual approach some people take. Do your due diligence prior to the event to find out as much as possible about its attendees, format, and etiquette. This will be time well spent, as you'll be prepared and confident when you walk through the door.

TALK TO EVERYONE

Once you're in the door, you're more than halfway there. Yet striking up a conversation with strangers can be challenging. To accomplish your goals, you have to leave your fear and your ego at home. Take a deep breath, be calm, and most importantly, be yourself. Inauthentic people can be spotted a mile away. No one wants to do business with someone they do not trust.

Networking is a two-way street. If you go in with an alternate attitude, you'll walk out empty-handed. Deals are rarely closed in a first meeting, unless your approach is to manhandle or bully your way through. You may get one or two sales with this method, but over time, your clients will see through this poor way of doing business.

Networking is about establishing relationships and staying connected to the people you meet. Walk into every event with the goal of building rapport and developing relationships, not just winning business. Ask simple questions, find a common interest, and be authentic.

BE READY TO LISTEN

While you may have an award-winning elevator pitch that's ready for the red carpet, it's important to be able to discern when you should talk and when you should listen. For example, if during a conversation someone mentions they need a contractor, share a recommendation. Right off the bat, you've done them a favor. You've solved a problem for them that had nothing to do with your business goals.

It's a simple lesson we learned in kindergarten: how to share. Share who you know and what you know. Don't be a hoarder of anything, whether it be your knowledge, your skills, or your network. This act of kindness will go a long way in opening up future conversations that may lead to new business.

FOLLOW UP

Following up is both an often-forgotten activity and the primary reason why business deals fall through. If you tell your newfound contact you will call them on Wednesday morning at 10:00 a.m., then guess what? Call them on Wednesday morning at 10:00 a.m. If you tell them you're going to email them information about your latest product offering on Thursday, then email them on Thursday. Want to score more points? Email it on Wednesday. Overdelivering is always better.

If you won't follow through on a simple email or phone call, how will this potential client know you will follow through if you do business together? Do what you say you will do, and if you can't, then contact the person well in advance to regroup. Don't wait until the last minute or give an excuse hours—or worse, days—later. By then, the damage is done, and you will need to work twice or three times as hard to repair what's been broken. Time does heal all wounds, but it will take a long time for trust to be restored.

Whatever the takeaway was from your encounter, phone call, email, or LinkedIn connection, deliver what you've promised. Remember, it's all about your integrity. You're building credibility with that person. Before long, they will begin to trust you. That trust is the foundation of any successful relationship, whether in business or your personal life.

TREAT PEOPLE WELL

It's important to never burn bridges and to treat everyone with kindness, respect, and generosity. That boss you disliked in your first fast-food restaurant job may very well be the perfect investor for your new project. That colleague you dissed in the weekly department meeting may one day lead your human resources department. There's a reason for every person you meet throughout your life.

After my retail facility manager experience ran its course, I stepped into a role with a large East Coast facility management company where I continued to hone my skills in sales and marketing. I regularly outperformed my colleagues, securing new clients and business all while maintaining trusted client relationships. I always under-promised and overdelivered because I saw what others were doing: promising the world and delivering nothing. I wanted to Be Better. My personal goal was to be known for my honesty and integrity. I apologized when I made a mistake and did all I could to fix it.

Treat everyone with the utmost respect, and you'll have no problem establishing solid professional connections that can transform into future clients or even employees.

KNOW WHAT YOU WANT

You have to identify what you want from these connections, so the people you reach out to know how to help you. "Do you have a job for me as a retail store sales manager?" is a much better question than, "Do you have a job for me?" "I'm starting a business and need a lawyer to complete my LLC paperwork" is much better than, "I'm starting a business and need help."

There has to be a purpose to your request to connect. The more specific you are about what you need, the better; otherwise, you're just wasting people's time, and if you don't get the help you need, you risk wasting your time as well. It's okay to not know what you don't know, but it's not okay to ask people for help without having some idea of the actual ask.

EXPAND YOUR HORIZONS

Many of us have relied on industry trade shows or conferences for the majority of our networking activities over the years. However, there may be smaller events or groups in your city you should consider adding to your list, as well as resources to help you launch or grow your business.

For example, consider checking out local Business Network International (BNI) meetings, Chambers of Commerce, or the Service Corps of Retired Executives (or SCORE Association). The Small Business Administration has a variety of resources available as well. Each of these should be thoroughly researched prior to investing a dime in business cards or office space.

Sometimes, our best connections are found in the most interesting places. Grocery stores, doctor's offices, and the gym are good places to practice your ability to make small talk, so don't pass up these opportunities. You may not find your next COO pumping iron, but these daily interactions keep your socialization muscles strong. While it can be difficult to put your phone away and strike up conversations, it is vitally important if you want to meet people who may one day play a part in helping you to achieve your goals.

DIVE INTO DIGITAL CONNECTIONS

Utilizing social media platforms, such as LinkedIn™, is vital to establishing and expanding your network. Now more than ever, these virtual connections are enabling us to continue to grow our businesses. Just as your first impression is key at a face-to-face meeting, so is the case online.

If you are not on LinkedIn, I urge you to join as soon as possible. This platform contains a wealth of information, as well as resources to help you find your next client or showcase your industry expertise.

To begin, ensure your profile is accurate and complete. Provide a great headshot and up-to-date information in all relevant sections, such as any volunteer work, awards, or other notable accomplishments. Seek out recommendations from former colleagues, clients, or business partners. Ensure you are well endorsed for your primary skills.

Next, spend some time—and I do mean a fair amount of time—connecting to people you know. Join applicable groups and follow companies, causes, and people that are in your industry or for which you have an interest. In short, make your LinkedIn profile as robust as possible so that when people view it, they get a clear and comprehensive picture of who you are.

If you're not particularly tech-savvy, hire someone to assist you. It will be money and time well spent to build your connections.

SPEAK UP

Once your profile is finalized and ready for prime time, make your voice known by posting meaningful content. This is not the place for pictures of your pets. It is a place to share information with your followers that you think they will find interesting and relevant. By posting regularly, as well as engaging with your connections, people will see you in their feeds and want to connect with you to get to know you better. It's a win-win for everyone.

Just like in-person networking is a give-and-take, so is virtual networking. Be sure to like, share, and comment on posts from your network. They'll appreciate the attention and pay it back to you. Spending 30 minutes each week on LinkedIn will pay dividends that can't be measured.

BECOME A THOUGHT LEADER

In addition to posting regular updates, if you are an excellent writer (or you can afford to hire one), periodically author articles on LinkedIn. Whether they address topics you are passionate about or simply offer insights into your industry, these articles will establish you as a thought leader. I encourage my team to post regularly, and their articles have led to new connections, as well as higher engagement on their profiles.

Establishing and growing a viable network both offline and digitally takes commitment. It also requires patience, as not every connection is going to turn into new business. In fact, it's better for your expectations to be lower to avoid frustration and disappointment. Focus on the process of building the relationship rather than gaining the signed contract.

BE GRATEFUL

One of the most important traits of any purpose-driven leader is gratitude toward everyone, including your network contacts. Whether they connected you with a potential client or were available to bounce ideas off of, they gave of their time and talent to help you.

These relationships, if properly fostered, will be invaluable to you as you grow your business or venture out into new projects. No one becomes successful on their own. Be thankful to everyone who has helped you in your business endeavors.

GUARD YOUR REPUTATION

If your goal for your entrepreneurial journey is to be more than a revenue generator, you must do more than turn a profit. Your character and integrity will speak louder than any industry award or accolade. Now more than ever, consumers and potential clients are watching the behaviors of leaders. They are doing business with companies that have a solid, authentic, and diverse company culture—not just a catchy tagline or cool logo.

Your reputation must be flawless. That's a weighty word, but I can't stress it enough. All eyes are on the CEO and the leadership team; therefore, ensuring everyone aligns with your vision is critical. People rarely give second chances, and when they do, it's with much trepidation.

When I began to formulate the plans for my business, I knew I'd have a handful of potential clients but would also need reliable subcontractors to actually do the work. I recognized it might be challenging to secure these key players as a newcomer in the industry.

Because of the relationships I'd fostered and the trust I'd built, many subcontractors gave me a chance. To this day, my company is known for treating our vendor partners well, and many have reached out to work with us. At the end of the day, we're nothing without our vendors. They are the ones in front of the client, our "boots on the ground." We need them as much as they need us.

This mutual respect between our vendors and my team results in our clients getting their work completed on time and on budget, which, in turn, results in satisfied clients who send us more business. I can't begin to tell you how critical word-of-mouth referrals are to a new business owner. A client or vendor is risking their own reputation when they send you potential business, so you must stay focused on service excellence.

Again, treat everyone with honesty and respect. These relationships, built and strengthened through purposeful networking, are why Branded Group has enjoyed exponential growth year over year since we launched in 2014.

BE PREPARED TO FAIL

Let's face it: we've all had those meetings that did not go as planned. Planes don't arrive on time. Traffic jams occur. I live in Orange County, California, so traffic is always a nightmare. Life happens, and guess what? It happens to all of us.

If that first impression was less than stellar, be straight with the other person and let them know you're sorry the meeting didn't go well. It's okay to be vulnerable and admit when things don't turn out the way you'd like. Own up to it and then give them your word that it won't happen again. Believe me, they'll appreciate your honesty and your desire to start over. Who knows? One day you may both laugh over that first encounter.

Don't be afraid to step out of your comfort zone from time to time. If you remember the best practices I've shared for being yourself—being generous with your time and talents, and being polite and respectful—you'll be light-years ahead of so many others in creating a network of clients and partners.

Networking is both an art and a science. The science is easy: there are a million books on how to be successful at networking. I encourage you to read them. However, the art of networking is up to you: it comes down to your creativity and your innovative approach to meeting and connecting with people. The better you know yourself, the easier it will be for you. Authenticity is the name of the game. Be yourself at all times.

If there's a character trait you possess that you don't like, change it. If there's a skill you need to improve, improve it. Every challenge has a solution if you're willing to seek it out. If you're going to lead a successful business, you need to be ready to face challenges, starting on launch day and on all the days that follow.

 To learn more about how to foster a grateful mindset, check out the *#BeBetter with Michael Kurland* podcast "Gratitude and a Side of Pasta" with Chris Schembra, Founder of the 7:47 Gratitude Experience™ and bestselling author of *Gratitude and Pasta: The Secret Sauce for Human Connection.* Go to MichaelKurland.co/bebetter-podcast.

CHAPTER 2

BE TEACHABLE

Asking for Help

My father was a workaholic, but even though he wasn't great at doing the "Dad" thing, he did instill a solid work ethic in me. In that way, he was my first mentor. He taught me that you don't have to be the smartest guy in the room or the one with the greatest ideas; if you're the person who outworks everyone else, you're going to shine. I've carried this mindset all of my life. I work hard at everything I do. If I'm in, I'm all in.

There are so many tasks you have to do when you start a business, and most of the time, you don't know what you don't know. For example, you might not know everything about filling out the required legal paperwork for your business entity, securing office space, and setting up an email system. Having an experienced business owner, a mentor, who can offer advice in these areas can jumpstart the initial stages of your business. Once you get past the startup phase, mentors can help with things like hiring, deciding if you should use cash or accrual accounting systems, or even figuring out payroll and payables.

Being teachable will help you avoid many common mistakes made by new business owners. Branded Group's success is due to the mentors I worked with before and during the initial days of my business. Their expertise and experience, as well as their connections to people who could help me, was invaluable.

I'd recommend having two to three mentors. More than that and you will be overwhelmed with all of the ideas and advice you'll receive. You know what happens when there are too many cooks in the kitchen.

Here are some practical tips on how to Be Teachable and find the best mentor.

FIND YOUR PERFECT MATCH

Who is your perfect match mentor? Most likely, it's someone you already know. They must have experience in doing what you want to do. Your mentor should be someone who is seasoned in the business you're seeking to launch or knowledgeable about the facet of your business that is not your strength.

I met my mentor, Bill Pegnato, through a friend. He was from the East Coast and, like me, also moved to California to open his business. We were both at a networking event and had similar stories—just a few decades apart. He pulled me aside and invited me to lunch.

Bill was looking to mentor someone—this is key. Not every successful business leader wants to be a mentor. It's time-consuming, and if you're trying to run your own business, it can be overwhelming to help someone else out. Therefore, be sure to seek out a person who has time for you and will be open and honest with you. You want a mentor who gets excited for you and has your best interests at heart. These trusted business partners will be an integral part of your success from the moment you sign the lease on your office space to the first day you turn a profit. They should be someone who will give you sound advice and who you can fully trust. If you don't trust their judgment, it's best to find an alternative.

However, even if your personalities are not 100 percent aligned in the early stages of the relationship, I caution you to not abandon ship too quickly. You may have to look past these "quirks," especially if the mentor has the expertise you're seeking. You should be open-minded as well as humble.

BE OPEN-MINDED

Don't be afraid to have frank conversations with your mentor about the expectations of your relationship. This is time well spent and may prevent potential frustration and confusion about each other's roles. Remember, you're not seeking opinions. You're seeking solid direction.

This will also require you to remain open-minded. Your mentor is going to offer you suggestions and advice, but if you're constantly pushing back, you're wasting their time and you may annoy them to the point where they won't want to help you. Be teachable.

GATHER AND PRIORITIZE YOUR QUESTIONS

In today's evolving business climate, it can be challenging for potential mentors to carve out time to coach and guide others.

Having a business plan with clear goals will help keep your time together focused on the goals you want to achieve. For example, if you are seeking to grow your client base in a new geographical region, conversations with your mentor will center on ways of accomplishing this task.

It's always fun and energizing to brainstorm new ideas for the business. However, in the early days, you need to be heads-down in the work that will get your business off and running.

As your business expands, you will have questions you did not anticipate, such as:

- How do I hire my first employee?
- What happens if I am audited?
- How do I pay my quarterly taxes?

Like any new business owner, you will have many questions that will pop up every day, but not all of them will need an immediate answer. Gather up your questions and prioritize them so you can use your mentor's time efficiently.

FIND MENTORS WITH COMPLEMENTARY SKILLS

A good mentor is an expert in their particular skillset, but no one is knowledgeable in everything. In the early days of my business, Bill helped me with operational tasks, including creating processes to manage our service calls more efficiently. Once my business was running smoothly, he and I began to discuss other challenges so that I could effectively scale my business.

While Bill was my go-to guy, there were others I reached out to when I needed assistance. I relied on my web designer to develop and update our website. I relied on our public relations firm for our brand-building projects. Your mentor may connect you to additional experts when your business hits certain junctures or milestones.

You can have more than one mentor, but be careful not to spread yourself too thin or get so many people involved that your head spins about which way to go.

UNDERSTAND YOUR RESPONSIBILITIES

In addition to respecting your mentor's time, there are other responsibilities you as a mentee should have. For example:

- Be on time, whether it's via Zoom, on the phone, or in person.
- Follow through on all of your commitments.
- Prepare an agenda to share with them prior to the meeting, including the goals of your time together and any action items you want to discuss.
- Develop thoughtful questions so they can gather any necessary resources that may be helpful.

Being responsible builds trust and proves to your mentor that you mean business and value their time.

EXPECT CHANGE

Speaking of time, how often should you meet with your mentor? The time commitment is going to evolve over the course of your business. In the beginning, it may be weekly, as there are several i's to dot and t's to cross. During the first couple years of Branded Group, Bill and I met quarterly. This changed to annually once the company was on a solid trajectory of growth.

The relationship changes over time. There will be times when you will look to your mentor for direction, and vice versa. Today, when Bill and I get together, we share updates about our businesses and we learn from each other. For example, I've discussed our successful social impact program, which inspired him to launch his own. Always be ready to give back to those who have helped you. In the early days, you're a taker, but as your business grows, remember to be a giver. I'm glad I was able to give something to Bill after all he'd done for me.

It may be hard to believe, but there will come a time when you will be ready to mentor others. If someone finds you at the right time and they have questions you can answer or they're seeking direction, be willing to share your experience with them. Be as helpful to them as your mentor was to you.

When your business is on a steady course, you may want to develop a mentorship program either for new hires or to develop promising leaders in your organization. As we hired people at Branded Group, I had an opportunity to lead my team in new ways. For example, we started a buddy program for new hires, as well as a coaching program.

Today, when a new team member starts their Branded Group journey, they are introduced to a dedicated colleague who answers all of their first-day questions and shows them the ropes. We specifically select the best people for this job because we want all of our new hires to feel welcome and to immediately be a part of the BeBetter team. I've experienced the benefits of having a mentor, and I know how powerful this relationship can be.

No successful entrepreneur succeeds alone.

 To learn more about my mentoring relationship with Bill Pegnato, check out the *#BeBetter with Michael Kurland* podcast "Launching a Business with Purpose" with Bill Pegnato, CEO of Pegnato Roof Intelligence Network. Go to MichaelKurland.co/BeBetter-Podcast.

CHAPTER 3

BE FEARLESS

Launching Your Business with Boldness

Fear of failure can be a great motivator.

I am inherently a risk-taker. However, I'm a risk-taker who does his research, whether it's about launching a business or jumping out of a plane. My approach to researching skydiving in 2019 was to avoid any "what could go wrong" stories. I wanted to have a positive mindset about this (perhaps) once-in-a-lifetime event. Maintaining a positive mindset allows me to be driven by fear rather than paralyzed by it. I've failed at few things in my life, and I realize the endeavors that didn't work out were probably not right for me.

When you decide to start a new business or expand an existing one, it can be scary—especially if you have never done it. You have to check your fear at the door; you have to be fearless. Being informed so you can make good decisions is just as important as not letting your fear get in the way. When it came to launching Branded Group, I was determined to succeed. I sold my home. I put every dollar I had into my company. I left my fear of rejection in New York as I made my way across the country. I was not going to fail.

If someone didn't want to do business with me, that was okay. There would be someone else. There would be another client, another partner. There always is if you're willing to persevere.

I was confident I could make it work because I had built authentic relationships throughout my entire career. My ability to connect to others made me stand out in all of my previous jobs. On my sales calls or client meetings, I never talked shop at the onset of the relationship. I focused on learning more about my potential clients and what was important to them. Of course, I wanted to make money, and at some point, I was going to ask for their business. It just wasn't going to be at the first meeting.

It can be scary to strike out on your own. I was an East Coast guy launching a business 3,000 miles away, not knowing a single soul professionally or personally in the area. But I did it, and the growth of my business is mind-boggling. Branded Group went from being an idea in my head in a small town on Long Island to a thriving, award-winning organization in Orange County, California.

Here are some practical tips on how to Be Fearless when launching your business.

KNOW WHO YOU ARE

Prior to launching Branded Group, I came to recognize a few things about myself that gave me the confidence to know I'd be successful starting my own business. First, I don't like having a boss. I don't like being told what to do or having my time dictated by someone else. If I could get away with something, I was going to try. I was going to push the envelope in order to achieve my goals, win clients, and advance my career. In short, I like freedom.

My resistance to authority doesn't mean I'm being rebellious and doing whatever I want whenever I want. That's irresponsible. As a CEO, employees and clients depend on me and trust that I know what I'm doing.

Just because there's no boss over you does not mean you can throw caution to the wind. Yet, there is freedom in how a goal is accomplished. For instance, with the rise of the virtual workforce, organizations of all sizes realized when their employees are focused on getting the work done—as opposed to getting it done between the hours of nine and five in the office—productivity can increase. People are more engaged.

Your team should be empowered to handle the responsibilities of the position. Your job is to be a coach, to be open to answering their questions or brainstorming new solutions to problems. The days of clocking in and out are long gone. Your focus and your team's focus should be on achieving your company's goals. The "how" is less important.

Knowing who you are as an entrepreneur will help you navigate these scenarios. It's not enough to have a good idea. It's not enough to have the capital to start a business. You have to know what makes you tick. You have to do some self-reflection and know your strengths and weaknesses.

DETERMINE YOUR "WHY"

In addition to discovering who you are as a business owner, you also have to understand why someone should buy from you. If you don't have an answer, it's time to go back to the drawing board because this lack of self-awareness and confidence may come back to haunt you. Without a firm sense of what you can offer, you won't be able to differentiate yourself from your competition.

Simon Sinek said, "People don't buy what you do; they buy why you do it." Our clients do business with us because we are focused on our "why," our purpose, which is to help "provide our clients with peace of mind and preserve their brand standards" through our BeBetter Experience. There are a lot of companies that can deliver the same services we do, but none deliver the BeBetter Experience. That comes from giving your team the freedom, the trust, and the tools to do their jobs.

My intention when I started Branded Group was to Be Better. Do facility management better. Do management of a team better. Do customer service better. Do giving back better.

The only way to achieve these goals was to stay true to my philosophy in every aspect of my business and hire people who aligned with this vision. When you hire for skills, you get worker bees. When you hire for cultural alignment, you get brand champions.

FILL A GAP IN THE MARKETPLACE

If you would've asked me when I was in college what kind of career I wanted to have, my answer most likely would've been something in sports. Launching a facility management business was the furthest thing from my mind. Yet, for more than a decade, I was in the retail facility management world, and that guided the natural progression of my career.

Right now, you might be sitting behind a desk wanting to start a business that is the exact opposite of what you are doing now. That's what makes being an entrepreneur so exciting—you can launch whatever business you want, whether it's a service or an actual product—but first, you have to become an expert in that industry.

I saw a gap in facilities management in California. Of the nearly 1,000 facility management companies in the United States, New York had about eight hundred. Other major cities across the country had approximately 50 or 60. If you looked at the number of retail corporate offices in 2014, New York had the number one spot. California had number two. So, my question was: why is no one opening up a facility management company in California?

I saw a gap, and I knew I could fill it. I had the skills, the drive, and the connections to get started. It's critical for new business owners to study their marketplace and identify any holes. Don't just copycat someone else; truly look to create your own niche. Otherwise, you'll spend all of your time chasing after the same clients as your competition.

My skills and strengths are in sales in the facility management industry. There was no sense in reinventing the wheel. I wanted to take all of my life's work and put it into my own company. I knew that most things I put my effort behind turned out successfully. Sure, it was definitely scary, but I felt confident in my abilities and I had a solid track record. There would be some bumps, but ultimately, I knew I would accomplish what I set out to do, which was to create a company that would Be Better.

DEVELOP A BUSINESS PLAN

For every entrepreneur, the first year of business is challenging. You are wearing multiple hats, and if you're on your own, you're wearing all of the hats. My co-founder, Kiira Belonzi, and I had two goals:

1. Get as many clients as soon as possible.
2. Don't go out of business.

After we both moved to California, we looked for office space and began to develop our business plan, which focused primarily on operations and sales. I knew I could bring in at least four clients. It turned out my thinking was pretty conservative. We tripled that number in our first days of business.

Many entrepreneurs think they don't need a business plan. It's intimidating, so it's understandable why many new business owners want to avoid writing one. However, at some point you're going to have to put something on paper, even if it's scratching out a budget on a cocktail napkin (keep that napkin!). You must have a vision for your business. It doesn't have to be a vision of where you're going to be in 10 years, but you have to at least know where you want to be when you open your doors.

If you don't organize your thoughts about your business, you're doing yourself a disservice. I'm a planner, but I'm not well organized. I tend to fly by the seat of my pants. As much as I would've liked to skip this step, I knew it had to be done. When you're in the startup phase, I recommend you plan for your first year. When you get through year one, focus on year two.

I don't think it makes sense to think about long-term planning as you're launching your business. There are just too many unknowns. It's important to have goals, such as revenue targets, but to plan five or 10 years during the startup phase is difficult.

You also need to be flexible and adaptable, as unexpected things will come up, both good and bad. Expenses you didn't plan for are just as possible as landing that big client ahead of goal, so you need to be able to course correct as needed. You have to know when to take risks, as well as when to spend your money more wisely.

For example, every year in the fall, we would begin to budget for the next year. We started with our sales estimates and identified what our expenses might be. When you're in startup mode, these line items likely include things such as rent, phone, internet, or office supplies. Depending on your business model, these will vary. A budget is nothing more than a detailed listing of monies coming in and monies going out; it's a road map of where you want to be and how you can get there. It's no different than a household budget. The key is to use this as a guideline, as opposed to something that must be adhered to exactly.

It's important to have a simple business plan and budget outlined to guide your actions and serve as your benchmarks in those first years of business.

SECURE FUNDING

You have your business idea. You have a short-term plan. Next, you have to make sure you have enough funding to run your business for a minimum of three to six months with no revenue. You have to be able to support the business financially; otherwise, you'll fail before you even get going.

Where does this funding come from? Today there are many options, including a bank loan or even a loan from parents or friends. These monies could come from your own savings, credit cards, or even a crowdfunding project. I sold my house and taxed my savings account to launch Branded Group.

LET GO OF YOUR EGO

This is something no one talks about when you start a business, especially if you are leaving a corporate or well-paying job to strike out on your own. You need to be prepared for the mental and emotional impact that taking a huge salary cut can trigger. If you're accustomed to bringing in a six- or seven-figure income with yearly bonuses or stock options, your ego may take a hit.

You can head off this potential shock by creating a personal budget before you launch your business, which is what I did. I needed to know how I was spending my money. I paid myself about $100 per week to cover my electric bill and have a couple of dollars in my pocket for gas and food.

Before you rent that office space or buy that new computer, be sure to keep some money to support yourself. You may not be able to get a paycheck, meaning during this lean time, you will have to be resourceful.

Also, if possible, prepay expenses like rent with your startup monies. You'll feel a big load off of your shoulders knowing you have a roof over your head if you face a negative cash flow for a time.

Remember, there will be no paycheck. There's no direct deposit every two weeks in those early days. I didn't pay myself until we were six months into the business; I didn't pay myself a real salary until around the middle of year two. But if you're prepared and practical, you can make it.

Focus on the fact that this deficit is only for a short period. You are setting yourself up for long-term success. Today, I'm happy to report that I am able to enjoy the fruits of my labors from those early days.

EVALUATE YOUR RELATIONSHIP WITH MONEY

It helps to think about your approach to managing money. If you have a scarcity mindset, you'll panic at every rejection. The first year in business, I had the mindset of "If I lose money, it's just money. I know how to make more."

As a business owner, you have to have this same mentality. You can't have so much anxiety about losing money that you make decisions out of fear. You have to take calculated risks and make decisions because they're the right decisions for the company. The short-lived pain of those early days of your business will be worth it in the long run. It may not be easy, but it is worth it when you see your dream coming alive. If you make a few sacrifices for your business initially, they will pay off exponentially as your business thrives.

DO YOUR RESEARCH

Many entrepreneurs will start their business in the town they reside in, which makes sense. I grew up in Norwalk, Connecticut, by the beach. I love the beach and have many fond memories of time spent there. It's my Zen place. When I had a bad day, you would find me at the beach, listening to the crashing of the waves. After college, I lived on Long Island, where pretty much every town is a beach town.

I knew I wanted my business and my future home to be on the beach. When I reconnected with a college friend who recommended I visit Newport Beach, I fell in love with the area and knew it was where I wanted to live and work.

Some might question this decision, since it made more sense to stay in New York. But remember, New York was already saturated with facility management companies and, if I wanted to differentiate myself, I had to go where there was opportunity.

That doesn't mean I didn't do some exploration ahead of time about the area and the state's laws for businesses to be sure it made financial sense. You can open your company wherever you want. However, I urge you to be smart about it. Do your research on business requirements such as state taxes or employment law.

BE HAPPY

Finally, consider where you want to be when you're *not* working. You're not going to be in the office 24/7, even though it might feel that way for the first couple of years. You will go home each night, and you want to go to a place that makes you happy.

"Be happy" is my response when I'm asked what the meaning of life is. It's very simple. There's so much unhappiness in the world. Doing things you don't love when life is so short just doesn't make sense to me. That's how I ended up in California. I'm really glad I made the move because now I'm able to enjoy the outdoors anytime I want.

 To learn more about how to launch a new business, check out the *#BeBetter with Michael Kurland* podcast "Pursuing Your Passions" with Kiira Belonzi, Co-Founder and Vice President of Business Development of Branded Group. Go to MichaelKurland.co/BeBetter-Podcast.

CHAPTER 4

BE PEOPLE-CENTRIC
Fostering Inclusivity

CONTRIBUTOR: KIIRA BELONZI

In the beginning days of Branded Group, our hiring process was mostly trial and error. Initially, we would hire anyone who had relevant experience and who would accept the salary we could offer them. For example, if someone had worked in a fire safety company, a related role in our industry, they'd likely be successful. If they had worked at a facility management company, that was even better.

The more we grew and learned, the more Kiira and I realized that knowing the facility management industry and possessing the "typical" hard skills were not necessarily required. Soft skills, such as being organized and being a good multitasker, were much more valuable. We also found being a good problem-solver and handling stress effectively would be beneficial, because the demands of this industry are many.

As a new entrepreneur, you will likely do the same. At first, you will hire people who will simply help you get the work done. However, eventually the primary tasks of each position will need to be identified so that you attract and retain the best talent. This might include thinking about what the job looks like on a daily basis. With this defined, you can start looking for those specific skills and desired character traits.

With this knowledge in hand, we began to look for people who were naturally well organized and who were self-starters. It was also important to find people who were comfortable and confident in making decisions. Once you teach people the skills they need to do the job, they have to be empowered to make decisions. It is not beneficial to micromanage. You have to prepare your team well then trust them to do their jobs.

Creating future leaders begins with hiring the right person for the job. You can teach almost anyone the job-related skills needed to be successful in a role. However, other skills such as the ability to be a team player and to step in when the need arises are part of a person's DNA, rather than a bullet point on their resume.

Creating an inclusive culture includes being able to recognize the strengths and talents of your team. Inclusivity means ensuring every voice in your organization is heard and everyone has equal opportunities to advance.

Here are some practical tips to Be Inclusive to build a diverse team.

ANALYZE HOW YOU'RE SPENDING YOUR TIME

Understanding which of your tasks need to be delegated is the initial step in figuring out who you should hire first. Consider doing a cost-time analysis to determine where your time is spent. Is what you are doing the best use of your time? The answer to this question will provide you with insights on when and who you need to hire.

When Kiira and I were starting out, I realized I needed to travel and do more selling face-to-face, leaving Kiira to run all of the service requests. We realized we needed to balance the workload as well as support the business's growth. If we couldn't get the work done, clients would leave.

We decided this would be a good time to hire our first employee. Soon, we had enough money to hire two people. However, I was still managing the finances. After traveling all week, I would reconcile our books and send out invoices. This was not an efficient way to handle this function because I wasn't a skilled bookkeeper. Yes, I could do it, but it was taking a long time, and more importantly, it was taking time away from securing new business.

If you're working with a partner or other team members, look at how they are spending their time too. Kiira and I analyzed how much time and effort she was putting in for various tasks. Then, we'd look at what I was doing to see how we could make it more efficient.

We were both trying to be fiscally responsible; perhaps we were *too* responsible and should've hired someone sooner. When to hire is a decision each business owner will need to make individually. It's important to know your numbers. You can't be negligent in this area. However, if your budget allows and you can bring in people to start taking on the work, it's worth it. There may be some additional upfront costs, but in the long term, it's the best investment to grow your business. Remember, your time is valuable.

IDENTIFY YOUR COMPANY'S GOALS

Having our new team members align with our culture was and is really important for us. We include our mission, vision, purpose, and core values on our website, so if a candidate did their research, they should know who we are as an organization.

To determine these critical guideposts for your organization, consider your responses to the following questions:

- **Purpose:** Why does your organization exist? Why does your organization do what it does? As Simon Sinek taught us, people don't buy what you do, they buy why you do it.
- **Mission:** How will you accomplish your "why"?
- **Vision:** Where will your organization be in five or 10 years? What do you want to accomplish?
- **Values:** What values will your organization adhere to in the face of adversity? What values are essential to supporting your team and your culture?

Your answers to these questions will set the tone for your company for years to come. Be sure to spend a fair amount of time on this exercise, as these statements will define your culture to your existing workforce and new hires. This is why in initial interviews, Kiira asks, "Why Branded Group? Why are you here?"

We want to find out what drew them to us and to the role. Nearly 99.9 percent of the time, the response is "I just love your culture," which has led to deeper conversations about what appealed to them and their reasons for wanting to join our team. If your company culture is not reflected on your website, described in a way that attracts top talent, put down this book and call your web designer right now. When a candidate can see your team in action and what it's really like to work for your company, chances are you'll attract the best person for the role.

If you have not defined your company culture but have done some soul-searching about the type of business climate you want, include it in your job description. You may not have a formal mission statement on your first day, but if you include information about your company's goals, this may be sufficient.

DEFINE THE SKILLS NEEDED FOR YOUR BUSINESS

The clearer you are on the skills needed for your business from the beginning, the more your team will thrive in their roles.

While we were refining our hiring process, Kiira and I did a fair amount of self-reflection. We evaluated our own character traits, strengths, and weaknesses. What made us successful? Which of these traits would we want in future employees? This exercise can be helpful for new business owners who don't have a pool of employees yet. As we began to build our team, we would evaluate the people on our staff who were doing well to help us home in on what we wanted for future hires.

The skills we were seeking are similar to what's required in many other jobs. Working independently and being a self-starter are pretty common skills, so we also ensured potential hires understood their responsibilities and what an average day would look like. We were transparent, especially with our first hires. We advised candidates that we would provide skills training, coach them as needed, and answer any questions. Afterward, we expected them to work independently.

While every role is going to require something different, there are key characteristics you want to look for in the candidates you're hiring. You want someone who is positive. In my mind, this is a must. No drama kings or queens! Any negative energy will zap your team of its motivation.

Humility is also important. One of our core values is **Be Humble**: approach every situation knowing there is always something new to learn. Being humble and teachable are critical in our culture. New hires should complement what you do, so they can fill the gaps of what you lack, but they shouldn't be arrogant or seek the spotlight. Everyone wants to be the boss, but there can only be one; otherwise, there's dissention in the ranks.

You need individual contributors who are committed to the company's success—people who are willing to work hard to get the job done. Another core value of ours is **Be Dedicated**: demonstrate loyalty to colleagues and clients. It's important to review the track record of potential hires. Do they jump from job to job after only a short time, or is there some sort of longevity? While it is now rare for people to stay in a job for decades, seeing a solid progression in their career paths can be a good indicator of their time with you.

Change is inevitable, and you need people on your team who are able to embrace and learn from it. We must be agile in order to face the ever-changing business climate and world events. Our **Be Adaptable** core value states that our team members must be able to approach change with flexibility and open-mindedness. They don't necessarily have to breeze through every situation, but they have to be able to stand strong, think clearly, and be good decision-makers and leaders.

Confidence is a must-have, but arrogance is something to avoid. You need to be mindful of people who come in and tell you they can fix all of your business challenges before they know what they even are. On the flip side, you don't want people who are timid and are afraid to share their ideas. These characteristics will be evident in an initial interview and will help you to figure out if they will be a productive team member. Monitor the conversation and watch body language to get insights into the candidate.

ASK THE RIGHT QUESTIONS

Sometimes, we discovered what character traits we needed simply through a gut feeling. Don't negate the importance of just "knowing." You might hear candidates say, "I like taking care of people" or "I like solving problems." Pay attention to remarks like this. How did the person look when they said it? Did they light up, or did it appear to be a rote answer?

Ask interviewees about their work style. Do they prefer to work independently or on a team? For example, an admin is given a list of things to do every day and they do them. The qualities you look for in a candidate for this role are different from what you'd seek in a customer service representative. An admin needs to manage their time well, to be quick and efficient.

A customer service representative needs to have people and problem-solving skills.

We'd also ask applicants about their prior experience and the culture of their previous jobs. For example:

- Do you prefer a large company to a small one?
- What did you like or dislike about either of these environments?
- What did you like or dislike about the company culture?

As of the writing of this book, Branded Group is no longer considered a startup or even a small business. We are also not a huge corporation. It's important to find out what the candidate prefers because this will determine how they will work with the team and the organizational structure. We are a diverse organization, and we strive to ensure everyone feels included, valued, and respected.

These initial interview questions were discovered by Kiira via an internet search. Since they were broad in nature, she went a step further to find questions that would help her evaluate candidates' specific character traits. She also avoided the simple "Yes or No" type of questions in order for the candidate to elaborate on responses and provide personalized responses. Generic questions will result in generic answers and will not be helpful in your selection process. Invest time to determine the best questions so that the interview will be fruitful for you and the potential hire.

A subtle clue as to the type of employee someone may be is how they prepared for the initial interview. Even if that first meeting is virtual, pay attention to how they present themselves. If they aren't willing to "dress the part" for the interview, what will they do when they are on the job? Did they do their research on your company? What questions are they asking? I know this might be an old-school mentality, but first impressions are still everything.

Even today, our first questions to candidates are "What do you know about Branded Group? What do you know about this position?" Their responses tell us how much they prepared for the interview but also what attracted them to the role.

I also pay attention to whether they showed up on time. If they are running late (which should be a red flag), did they call? Is it a legitimate reason or is it flimsy? We all need to be flexible and understanding, but it's important to pay attention to these simple actions because they may very well spell success or failure for that employee.

Always check references. Always. If a candidate doesn't have any, that's concerning. Everyone can find someone to provide a letter of recommendation, even if it's a teacher or a coach.

EVALUATE YOUR INTERVIEWING SKILLS

There's an art and a science to interviewing.

So, what if you're not the best interviewer? Frankly, if you're a solopreneur, you'll have to get better at this skill. But if you have a partner, then consider delegating this task to them.

While you want to "sell" the company to the potential hire, you also want to be sure you're being upfront about the position. If it's a fast-paced environment, describe it as so. If it requires long hours, say that. It has to be right for both the company and the candidate. Otherwise, you'll find yourself looking for their replacement.

It's important to avoid monopolizing the conversation. Be open to hearing what the candidate has to say. If you're the one doing all the talking, then you're not going to get the information you need. Everyone might feel good afterward because you had a great conversation, but did you learn anything about the candidate? Did you just give a sales pitch, leaving both you and the candidate with unanswered questions?

We were hiring for several entry-level positions in those first few years. The candidates did not have much experience, yet when Kiira interviewed them, she was able to refine the questions so they could share their applicable skills or experience. For example, when asked about their problem-solving skills, one candidate shared how they helped cochair committees at their high school. Problem-solving is problem-solving, right? If they have the aptitude and the motivation, the actual experience may not be as important. Once you break the ice and get the candidate talking, you will better understand their character, their personality, their abilities, and their future potential.

People have different interviewing styles, and it's important to adjust so that you can get a complete picture. If you're on edge, the applicant will be too. Consider talking about the weather or traffic to put them at ease. You do have to ask the hard questions, but you don't have to lead with them.

Kiira is a conversationalist. She makes people feel comfortable right away and secures information that helps us hire the best people. If two people are equally skilled, she can evaluate their answers to some of the softer questions to help in the selection process.

Don't forget to take notes, even if it's only a few words or short phrases. These will help you differentiate one candidate from the next. After they leave, be sure to record any additional insights or important points.

REFINE THE ONBOARDING PROCESS

Retention begins with a solid onboarding process that is continuously refined as your business grows and you better understand the needs of your employees, as well as the roles for which they were hired. Our new hire training and onboarding process has evolved over time, and today we have a program that sets up every one of our team members for success.

What is a successful onboarding process? For starters, it includes how you welcome new team members. People spend more time at work than they do with their family. You want them to enjoy being a part of the team. Since we transitioned to a fully remote workforce, we had to change some of our new hire processes and do a few things differently. For example, we send all new hires a care package filled with office supplies and company swag. It's been a big hit, and everyone has commented on how it made them feel welcome.

We also schedule ice-breaker meetings, which give our new team members the opportunity to meet some of their colleagues, including leadership. These informal gatherings help them to put faces to names as well as establish connections to people they may not interact with on a daily basis.

We also hire in groups, even if it's just two or three people. We do this for a few reasons. Until you hone your hiring process, you might want to hire two people for the same role. This way, if one of them leaves, you won't have to repeat the process. Evaluate what went wrong, but don't take it personally. Rather, ask yourself, *Could I have trained them better? Was there something I missed in the interview?* This is why our hiring process has continually been refined: we learn from each situation.

If both hires are equally skilled, it works out even better because as your business grows, you may want to consider "hiring ahead." While there may be some added upfront expense, it will be worth it in the long run.

The other reason we hire multiple people simultaneously is to onboard them together. There's a built-in camaraderie among new hires when they all start on the same day. They share a common bond throughout their time on the job. Today, our onboarding program is completely virtual. We have implemented innovative practices to foster community among our new hires.

Shortly after a new team member is on board, we offer them the CliftonStrengths tool. This assessment has been a game changer. When I interviewed people, I always asked them about their strengths so we could put them in the best role. This wasn't always a slam dunk, and we did get it wrong sometimes, but some of those "wrong roles" paved the way for better ones.

In fact, we have multiple examples of people who changed roles within the organization. For example, we had someone move from an administrative role into our IT department, and she's done an amazing job with our technology.

I recall another instance where one of our salespeople was struggling. I decided to take her to lunch to find out why. We discussed her previous role in another company, where she managed a department. I told her we needed someone to do the same for us and offered her the opportunity.

She took the weekend to think about it and decided to accept the new role. Today, this department rocks! I don't even have to think about it anymore. A function that was once a source of angst for everyone is now flourishing.

INVEST IN YOUR EMPLOYEES

The more you invest in your employees, the faster your company will grow.

If I could change anything about the launch of Branded Group, I would've put more effort into developing a training program. This might've been challenging because I didn't know exactly what we needed. Yet, if you know what to expect from each role, you can build a job description detailing how that job actually works. Afterward, you can start working on a training plan to skill people up.

I realize this seems like something to do once you have a solid P&L and a healthy sales funnel, but your employees are the lifeblood of your company. When they are equipped with the resources and tools to do their jobs, they'll become highly productive. We have fine-tuned our training program over the years, and it's resulted in our team members becoming more confident in their skills.

While I'm not suggesting you need to have your entire training program in place or all of your job descriptions completed when you open your doors, the faster you can iron out these tasks, the faster you will begin to experience the success you envisioned. If you have a simple plan in place, you can hire people who have the skills you're seeking then teach them the other skills they need. If you have a dedicated team member to conduct this training, that's even better.

KNOW WHEN AND HOW TO LET SOMEONE GO

By now, you understand the importance of knowing when to hire, who to hire, and why onboarding and training are key to their success. But what if, after all of your investment of time and energy, it's just not working out? What if your attempts to repurpose people into a different role fail? If this is the case, it's time for some hard decisions to be made.

Sometimes you have to let people go. It's a scary thing, especially if you've never fired someone. It can be intimidating, but you will inevitably have to do it eventually. Sometimes, you just have to do it for the health and well-being of the organization. If someone is not right for your organization—or worse, is wreaking havoc—it's best for all involved that they move on.

Don't let a sense of guilt keep you from doing what's best for your company. If you have exhausted every option to help them succeed and it's still not working out, it is time to take action. More than likely, the person will find something else and be just fine. If you handle the process professionally and legally, it won't be fun, but it will be for the best.

I don't take this topic lightly. I have learned a lot of lessons about personnel management. As a CEO, I know this job is someone's livelihood. I know I provide the salary that pays their mortgage or their childcare. If someone is not excelling in their role, there's a reason. Perhaps they are in a job that doesn't maximize their skills. If they are a productive team member, it is worth my while to have an open and honest dialogue to see if another position may be better for them.

Alternatively, what if an employee decides to leave? This is a risk for any business owner. Most of the time, you did not do anything "wrong." We no longer live in a time or culture where people stay in jobs for 30 years. People rarely stay in the same city for that long, let alone the same job. People leave jobs for many reasons, and the best thing you can do as their leader is to wish them well, offer to write letters of recommendation, and thank them for their service to you.

TREAT YOUR EMPLOYEES WELL

What if instead of a weak team member, you have a rock star? In my previous jobs, I ran circles around everyone—not because I was smarter, but because I worked harder, which is why I earned promotions and raises.

I want people who are going to go above and beyond. I'm not looking for someone who just wants to do the bare minimum and get promoted because they've been with us for a certain amount of time. That doesn't fly with me.

But when I see an employee doing more than their fair share, seeking out opportunities to learn or asking to be on project teams, that's a sign of leadership. Whenever possible, try to fill roles from within your team because these are the people who are loyal. Always look to prepare your team members to take on the next big role. Healthy employee engagement and retention stats come when people are in the right job that matches their skills, talents, and work preferences.

This is one of the best features of Branded Group: we have the right people in the right jobs. If they weren't in the right position on their first day, we took notice, had a conversation, and made a way for them. It's important to invest time into your hiring and training programs. When you have a team that's functioning cohesively, it helps your bottom line and also strengthens your company culture.

I encourage you to hire the best people you can afford for every stage of your growth. Remember, you will be relying on them very heavily in the early days. At first, they will simply lighten your load. As time goes on, they can take on more responsibilities so that you can focus on the growth of the company. If you play your cards right and hire the best people, they will also have ideas to help your business flourish.

You might not be able to afford to hire people full time due to the cost of expenses like benefits and insurance—that's okay. There are many ways you can secure the help you need without hiring a full-time staff. Be creative! To start, you can hire consultants or part-time people. When we launched Branded Group, we hired consultants to fill several roles.

Reach out to your professional network. Talk to your clients. Ask your mentor if they know anyone. There are many people who can help you run your business if you're willing to seek them out.

These days, we know what we want in a candidate. In this industry, we need someone who can handle the pressure of prioritizing tasks, who is well organized, and who wants to be a part of a purpose-driven organization. We're not looking for warm bodies anymore. We're looking for the right attitude, someone who's going to come in and support their colleagues and do the best job they can for our clients. We are also looking for people who want to participate in our social impact programs and contribute to our culture.

As your business grows, you will continually fine-tune your hiring process, training programs, and onboarding procedures. Your team is key to your success. These investments in time— and possibly money—will pay off, and you will attract and retain top talent who will be a great source for referrals.

 To learn more about how you can build a culture that is engaging and inspiring, check out the *#BeBetter with Michael Kurland* podcast "Building Sustainable Inspiration Within Company Culture" with Allison Holzer and Sandy Spataro, Co-CEOs of InspireCorps. Go to MichaelKurland.co/BeBetter-Podcast.

CHAPTER 5

BE FUTURE-DRIVEN

Navigating Organizational Growth

Your business needs to be future focused, even before you have your entire team in place.

As Kiira and I expanded Branded Group, we were able to afford to hire people who had more experience. This was when we brought in our president, Jon Thomas. Kiira was the training expert, I was the sales and marketing expert, and Jon became the operations expert.

There will come a time when your business grows enough that you will need to separate your employees into functional areas or teams. At first, we were one big team, and everyone did what needed to be done. It was all hands on deck. However, this is not sustainable as you continue to add clients and employees. People will begin to step on other people's toes, and there will be duplication of effort. Inefficiency will be the name of that game.

When we began to see this happening, we tasked Jon with reorganizing everything. He put smaller teams in place that were focused on a particular industry vertical. This client-driven approach aligned with the client needs, because we found they preferred communicating with the same person when they called, which strengthened the relationship.

Jon is a big proponent of continuous improvement, and our internal operations are always being evaluated to squeeze out every last bit of efficiency. He can easily see where a process is broken and quickly fix it. He will also break processes on purpose and encourages his team to as well, so he can make it better.

Here are some practical tips on how to Be Bigger while navigating organizational growth.

HIRE THE EXPERTS

As your business grows, a solid team will enable you to begin removing some of the hats you wore as CEO. After about six months of nonstop activity, Kiira and I were ready to hire.

Most entrepreneurs are opening their businesses in the state where they reside and have connections right around the corner. However, Kiira and I had moved across the country and knew no one. We didn't have a local network of friends or colleagues. It was all new territory.

We spent a lot of time searching résumés on a variety of employment websites. Our first hire had some experience in the industry and was within our budget. As we added more people, we invested time and energy into training. They were good team players and had the traits we wanted, but they lacked the industry knowledge and skills we needed.

At this time, Kiira and I were both reading *The E-Myth: Why Most Small Businesses Don't Work and What to Do About It* by Michael Gerber. This is an amazing book that will help you identify the type of business owner you are so you can understand how to manage and delegate tasks to your team. The book dives into the importance of hiring experts, which is what we did when we hired our CPAs, lawyers, and insurance agent. We did not take shortcuts because we knew if we didn't hire the best people, we'd have to hire someone to fix their mistakes, potentially costing us more money.

This same principle applies when hiring your first employees. Your gut is telling you to keep costs down because you're trying to grow your business, but hiring the wrong people will end up costing you more.

BE FAIR AND GENEROUS

Your sales team is the bread and butter of your business. This is not to say other functions are not critical, but without a healthy funnel of client prospects coming in, there's not much for the rest of your team to do. Building trust with your sales team, being fair with commission payouts, and recognizing everyone for their part in the sales process creates a cohesive and unselfish team.

"Unselfish" is not a word you hear much in the world of sales. In my previous sales roles, my commissions were kept from me and placed in the "house account," even though I closed the sale and serviced the account. Conversely, in other positions, I was freely paid the commissions I earned. My point is that the sale, no matter who secures it, feeds the entire company's bottom line.

Pitting team members against each other or withholding commissions is a surefire way to demotivate employees and cause animosity. To this day, even if I get a lead, I give my team the commission. They're the ones running the account and growing it. They're spending their time deepening the relationship.

Your people want to feel that they are valued and appreciated. Don't be stingy with their commissions. It sparks a culture of distrust, and eventually, it will impact your entire team.

LOOK FOR SHARED VALUES

Today, our hiring process is so refined that I don't need to be involved. Our Human Resources Department and other team members do the vetting and hiring. Our hiring goals are dramatically different. Today, we look for critical skillsets required for our industry, such as organization, time management, and customer service.

We also evaluate personalities during the interview process and ask relevant questions to get to know them, such as:

- Does this person have a positive outlook?
- Are they confident?
- Do they do well under stress?
- Do they have good energy?
- How do they handle multiple tasks or deadlines?
- Could they align with the Be Better culture?

We have spent much time and effort building an upbeat, positive culture, and we want our team to embrace and reflect that to our clients. Our employees consistently rate us highly in this area on our annual employee engagement survey, noting how they feel connected to their team members and that we are being true to our vision.

LEARN FROM THE LITTLE MISTAKES

In the beginning, we made some mistakes, but that's to be expected for any new business owner. For example, we were not aware of the paperwork that was needed for our employee files, and Kiira had to do a fair amount of work to ensure we were in compliance. The key is to learn from these mistakes, create better processes, and get crystal clear on the type of employees you want to have working for and with you.

We tried to keep our mistakes to a minimum. You can't make catastrophic mistakes! If you're an entrepreneur, that's goal number one. Everything we did wrong, we learned from, and everything that we did right, we built upon.

BALANCE YOUR TEAM

My strengths are in sales and marketing; therefore, I'm all about building relationships. This serves me well when coaching my team. Yet, even if you are a great relationship builder, it can be challenging to balance all of your team's different personalities and needs.

Everyone has different professional goals: some want to move up the ladder while others are happy being individual contributors. You have to be able to understand your team's skills and talents so that they can seamlessly collaborate.

Our attention to putting processes and programs into place helps Branded Group run smoothly. That's not to say we don't have a hiccup from time to time, but when I travel or take a vacation, I know I won't get calls in the middle of the night about an issue. I no longer have to sweat the small details. My management team handles the daily operations, and I can focus on the strategic vision for the company.

I am able to take my foot off the gas a little bit here and there, and I can actually be a full-time CEO, wearing one hat instead of many. For example, in addition to my sales role, I was also once responsible for client billing and finance functions. It's been a journey since I traveled across the country to where we are today—a journey that didn't happen overnight. This process took sacrifice, courage, and a dose of unselfishness. However, if you put in the work, you will see results.

Today, we have an organization that runs relatively seamlessly, and in my humble opinion, the BeBetter team is second to none.

 To learn more about how to build a high-growth company, check out the *#BeBetter with Michael Kurland* podcast "How to Create an Award-Winning Culture by Putting People First" with JeVon McCormick, President and CEO of Scribe Media. Go to MichaelKurland.co/BeBetter-Podcast.

CHAPTER 6

BE PURPOSEFUL

Creating Brand Champions

Earlier in my career, I was seen as replaceable. Maybe you feel the same way. I was a commodity. I was a line item on a P&L that was costing the company money. Sure, I was climbing the ladder, but it wasn't fun. At my yearly reviews, I'd get a paltry raise, even though I was giving 110 percent and bringing in the majority of new business.

What my previous employers should've been doing was recognizing and valuing my efforts as one of their top salespeople. You have to ensure your team feels valued, that they know their contributions are making a difference, and that you care.

In my company, we treat our employees well. I know what it feels like to not be valued, and I did not want my team to feel that way. I aim to create an atmosphere where people feel cared for and cared about. Of course, everyone is going to want to be paid well and get raises, but top talent is looking for more than money. You will be able to attract and retain people if you have a thriving company culture. The keys to engagement and retention are inclusion, appreciation, flexibility, and trust. At Branded Group, we want to create brand champions, and that starts with being purposeful about the employee experience.

Here are some practical tips to Be Purposeful and create brand champions.

DEFINE CORE VALUES

Even before you are fully staffed, you can take steps to keep your existing employees engaged with their work and your business goals. If your hiring process did its job, you should have motivated people who are ready to contribute to the organization's success as well as their own. However, even motivated people can quickly become disengaged if you have not defined your company's core values. Without a set of core values, your employees won't know what's expected of them.

This is another reason to look beyond the skillsets of potential hires during the interview process. If you hire solely for what's on their résumé, which I think is a very 1980s way to hire, they will get the job done, but that's about it. If you don't have a strong culture, your employees will be disengaged and you will have a staff of clock-watchers instead of team members who are helping your business grow.

I've seen many organizations that don't have an engaging company culture, and in most cases, it's because of the leader. They are the biggest problem. They don't roll up their sleeves when needed. They bark out marching orders to their team. They're disorganized. These actions discourage their staff and lower morale. How can your employees rally around you as their leader if you're not being a good example of your core values?

I believe the single most important thing you can do as a business owner and CEO is to define the core values of your company. These guideposts should reflect your team's feedback. For Branded Group, one of our core values is to Be Altruistic, which is at the heart of our organization. We give back. We want to make a difference. We want to change lives. Because giving back is rooted in our culture, we ask candidates about it in our interview process. While we would never force anyone to join us in our social impact activities, we want a team that is motivated to help others, not just to collect a paycheck. This is why we gathered input from our team in the creation of our vision, mission, and core values. We wanted to find out what was important to them. We live and breathe our core values, and as the CEO, I lead by example.

MAKE CULTURE MORE THAN WORDS ON A WALL

Branded Group's vision is to "build a conscious business to inspire future humanitarian leaders." This vision permeates everything we do, from our hiring processes to professional development to employee feedback. Our social impact program volunteer activities offer opportunities for meaningful team interactions, which is reflected in our employee engagement survey results year after year. We receive high marks for adhering to our purpose to "provide our clients with peace of mind and preserve their brand standards through our BeBetter Experience."

Your company culture has to be evident in all you do. Relying on an annual picnic or holiday party to get the message across is not going to cut it if you're looking to engage and retain a loyal workforce. But when you live and breathe your vision, your team will too.

Whether I'm slinging a hammer at a Habitat for Humanity home build project, running in a company-sponsored 5K, or picking up trash on our beaches, I'm standing behind our core values. I'm not afraid to get my hands dirty, and my actions match my words.

CREATE A POSITIVE CULTURE

Over the years, many friendships have formed within our organization. Our team enjoys working together. They go above and beyond because they are engaged relationally with their colleagues.

As you know, it costs more to win a new client than it does to retain an existing one. The same holds true for your employees. Think about the time and money you spend on your hiring and training. Also think about the opportunity cost of this task. If you're hiring and training new people all of the time, what is *not* getting done because you don't have the manpower?

However, if you're investing in your existing team by providing job skills or leadership training, they're becoming rooted in your business. Their loyalty is deepened. It's even better when they can serve as mentors or coaches to new hires or those looking to move up the career ladder.

Clients also prefer working with the same people. They don't like it when their account reps or customer service reps keep changing. Therefore, when your employees are happy, your clients will be happy and relationships will deepen, which is especially important in our industry. Sure, there's always going to be someone who's dissatisfied, but if the majority of your team is engaged and feels valued and appreciated, you're doing something right.

As a leader, whether you are a CEO or a supervisor, if you see that one of your team members isn't thriving, you owe it to yourself and them to find out why. Don't avoid these tough conversations because you don't like confrontation. It may be as simple as a work-life alignment issue and they need some flexibility with their schedule. Or, it could be that they are in the wrong role.

This is why assessments like CliftonStrengths and others can be so valuable. By finding out where people are gifted and where their skills are the strongest, you can place them in the best positions. If you can transition them into a new role and give them the opportunity to learn and grow, it's a win-win. They're more engaged, and you've essentially given them a fresh start because you were willing to have an honest exchange about their role. When you show you care about the whole employee, you create loyal brand champions.

ASK WHAT YOU CAN CHANGE

Another way to improve engagement levels and retention rates is to survey your employees. When you do this does not matter. Whether you ask 10 questions or 50 does not matter. There just needs to be a mechanism where people can actually share their thoughts with you.

Some of you may remember the suggestion box in the break room from years ago. Today, the same concept has been digitized and transformed into online surveys. A simple questionnaire can provide a glimpse into what your team is truly feeling about your organization, their role, and even your culture.

A word of caution: if you have no plans to put their feedback into action, it may be wise to reconsider whether you need to ask the question. For example, if you feel you have the best benefits package you can afford, do not include questions about how you can make your benefits better. If you can't give people more time off, do not ask if they are satisfied with your PTO policy.

Our culture is one of transparency and honesty. Be Honest is another one of our core values, which is why we share all of the results with our team—*all of them*. In the beginning, the feedback we received was tough to take. Yet because of it, we made changes to our internal communications, our vacation policies, and even our after-hours coverage.

There were many ideas shared that we were not able to implement right away, so we explained why we couldn't. As a result, our staff did not think their ideas or concerns were being ignored. We told the truth. We could not expect our team to uphold our core value of honesty if we as senior leaders withheld information. This approach has deepened the trust in our organization.

Know that you will not be able to make all of the people happy all of the time. You have to be able to take criticism and negative feedback. Put your ego aside, be humble, and ask yourself if the feedback is true. Is it being shared by one person, a handful, or is it a systemic problem? Once you determine the commonalities, you can brainstorm ways on how to improve.

Since our first employee survey years ago, we have acted on many of the suggestions, which lets our team know they have been heard. They see how their voice matters and how they are a meaningful part of the company. Today, because we are in a state of continuous improvement, we often have programs and policies in place before they're raised in these surveys.

Our commitment to our team has positively impacted our engagement and retention rates over the years. While there are many things that can impact these important indicators of your company's overall health, having an exceptional culture is the foundation. If your retention or engagement are in flux, it might be worthwhile to look at the training you offer or your business operations. These or other processes may be in need of an overhaul so that you can help people be more productive and efficient in their jobs. It might be a big issue, like how you communicate with your team. It could be a problem fixed with something as simple as an employee recognition program. Either way, addressing factors impacting your culture will directly affect your team's morale and motivation.

As your company evolves, these facets of your business will need to be continually reevaluated. What worked in your first year won't work in your fifth. It's really about being agile. You have to be able to adjust and course correct as your business grows.

Our team is invested in our success because our culture is

strong. As a leader, I am invested in the vision, purpose, mission, and core values of my company. You too will have to be invested. This is what Be Better leaders do.

Good leaders rally people for a common cause. They will be your brand champions. They will be the ones who help make your entrepreneurial dream a reality. Be purposeful about investing in your employees, whether it be through professional development or launching a wellness program, so you can show them that they are vital to your organization. As leaders, we must do all we can to show our teams they are respected, cared for, and valued. Without them, your business will not be successful.

 To learn more about how to spark inspiration in your culture, check out the *#BeBetter with Michael Kurland* podcast "Four Ingredients to a Lasting Company Culture" with Dr. Tracy Brower, Vice President of Workplace Insight at Steelcase and author of *The Secrets to Happiness at Work* and *Bring Work to Life by Bringing Life to Work*. Go to MichaelKurland.co/BeBetter-Podcast.

CHAPTER 7

BE ENGAGING

Building a Culture with Longevity

Before I launched Branded Group, I was struggling with a number of health challenges. A broken foot derailed all meaningful physical activity. I also formed several poor habits, which contributed to a 50-pound weight gain. Because of my foot injury, my back has always been misaligned, and even today, it flares up from time to time. These challenges, along with losing my full-time job, contributed to a depressed mindset and a lack of motivation to do anything about it.

I knew if I wanted to accomplish my dreams, I had to make a change—several changes, actually.

New habits start with a decision to make a change. Perseverance and commitment make habits stick. Bad habits arise when we lose that commitment or simply quit. There's really only one way to reverse the trend: make a decision to change and put a plan in place, being mindful of distractions or naysayers that try to derail your success.

To get out of the hole I was in, I began pursuing a healthier lifestyle. I cleaned up my eating habits and started an exercise program. Over a period of time, I lost the weight and found a passion for working out daily. Whether this includes a trip to the gym, walking the dog, working out on my Peloton™, or participating in my company's various volunteer events, such as the 5K, I am committed to this lifestyle.

I'm not suggesting CEOs have to be bodybuilders, but they do need to pay attention to their health and mental well-being because many people are depending on them. Employees, clients, vendors, and colleagues want to know you are doing all you can to remain at the helm. I want to Be Better for myself, but I also have a growing workforce that relies on me. I need to be around for them.

I had to put good habits into place that I could follow through on every day. It's a lifestyle—it's not a quick fix that's implemented just to deal with the crisis of the day. A diet will give you immediate results, but it will take a true investment in your wellness to bring about lasting changes. Exercising, meditating, and practicing daily gratitude are some of the ways that I live a well-balanced life.

While it is important to develop a healthy mindset for your personal wellness, it should translate into your business. Creating a culture of wellness in your business requires the same level of commitment. When you create a culture centered on a healthy mindset, the investment will pay off in the long run.

Here are some practical tips to Be Engaging in creating your company culture.

CREATE A CULTURE OF EMPATHY

Every organization has gone through a myriad of changes in the past few years. I saw firsthand the toll that some of these events took on my colleagues and team members. This heightened awareness led me to more fully understand the importance of compassion and empathy. Everyone struggles on some level, and the ability to put yourself in someone else's shoes for just a moment changes your personal perspective and deepens your relationships.

When employees feel valued and truly cared for, they will give you their best. However, if they are experiencing a lack of compassion or feel they are not appreciated, they will seek other opportunities. That's what I did.

I recall a performance review when I was working in the industrial cleaning equipment industry. I expected a big raise because I had hit my sales goal. Instead, I was given excuse after excuse for why I wasn't going to get it. No matter how I tried to convince my supervisor that I deserved this money, he wasn't budging. I was just a number to him. I was overhead. Feeling utterly deflated, I went home that night, brushed up my résumé, and started my job search. The only goal of that company was to make money. So, when people weren't making money or felt cheated out of what they deserved, they left.

INVEST IN YOUR EMPLOYEES

The "sunk costs" of both losing people and recruiting new hires is high. Think about how much it costs you to hire and train someone from day one to when they are fully independent. The onboarding process may take only a few months, but for employees to feel confident in their role, it can take up to a year. If you were investing in the stock market for 12 months, wouldn't you want a healthy return when you sold your stock? You certainly wouldn't want your advisor to tell you that your money didn't grow, or worse, that you lost it all.

Your return on investment is based on the stocks in which you invest. The same is true for your employees. Your return on investment in them is based on the company culture you've invested in. If you've done it right, your company becomes a welcoming environment that your team wants to be a part of. Many of our team members rely on their colleagues as their primary support network. Providing a place where they can be nurtured, accepted, and supported in their careers was important for me to create.

Identifying your company culture from the launch of your business helps you remain true to your vision. When you have this vision, all of your future decisions can be made more easily, whether those decisions are about hiring employees, developing a wellness program, or securing new clients. A culture rooted in a clear vision is sustainable through the various cycles of your business. Our culture is the heart of all we do. Our Be Better philosophy is not just words we put on a screen saver or add to a social media hashtag. Everyone embraces it, and it binds us together.

MAKE YOUR VISION COME ALIVE

When I started Branded Group, I wanted to create a company with an outstanding culture. I wanted to make it a place where people wanted to spend their time. If you enjoy where you are working, you will want to stay, and you will encourage others to join you because you're fully engaged and you love your work.

In many organizations, employees don't feel comfortable talking to the CEO. There's a hierarchy and a perceived "classism" that can prevent relationships from forming. I never wanted a culture like that. Yes, I am the CEO, but I want to have an atmosphere where my team and I can talk about sports, hobbies, or whatever topic they're interested in. I want to be relatable. I don't want my team to be intimidated and feel like they can't talk to me.

From the first day, we had the simple goal to treat our employees, clients, and vendors better. Because of our collective experiences at our previous companies, Kiira, Jon, and I were determined to build a better workplace where everyone was valued. Honesty and integrity would drive our relationships. We would do what we said we would do, and we would keep our promises.

This is the opposite of the cultures my executive team and I had experienced at past jobs. While a healthy bottom line was and is important, without a solid culture, all you are doing (hopefully) is making money. You're not making a difference. I wanted to show my team that it wasn't just about the money. We turned a profit our first year, but I wanted to do more. I wanted to leave a legacy.

I wanted a workplace where people liked coming to work, even looked forward to it. I wanted them to be happy to be there. I wanted them to feel confident and comfortable talking to supervisors about their ideas. There's nothing wrong with making money—I simply wanted more, and I believe our employees wanted more too. Most of my staff is made up of millennials who are looking for more than a paycheck. They want to work for a company that stands for something, that gives back to their community.

The facility management industry is not glamorous. It's nonstop phone calls, troubleshooting, and managing clients and vendors 24/7/365. The fast pace can sometimes lead to high turnover. It's not uncommon to see a new face every week in this industry.

Because of our company culture, I've been privileged to have long-term employees who are happy and productive. They're not clock punchers waiting for the 5:00 p.m. whistle. In fact, quite the opposite is true, which is why we have been certified as a Great Place to Work® year after year.

PROVIDE WELLNESS RESOURCES

To keep our team focused on physical and mental health, we routinely include wellness topics and resources in our monthly newsletter, such as meditation apps, journaling resources, and healthy recipes. Additionally, many of our giveback initiatives revolve around physical activity. For example, we've held multiple 5K events benefiting local organizations and have built or restored homes for Habitat for Humanity.

Many of our employees have quit smoking, lost weight, or started a yoga practice. Each has found what works for them, and we support their efforts.

SECURE REGULAR FEEDBACK

Company culture is not created overnight. It's always evolving and growing. You do, however, have to have a vision of the kind of culture you want and what will make sense for your organization. Branded Group's culture will not work for anyone else because it's unique to us.

Our culture is rooted in our mission, vision, purpose, and core values. Our team members had input into these components of our company culture, giving them a sense of ownership about them. They now have skin in the game, and this is why many of our employees have been with us for so long.

Annual employee engagement surveys helped us to continuously improve our culture because we listened to and acted on the feedback from our team. Processes were refined and programs were implemented to address the gaps.

Employee surveys are an integral component in a strong culture. Having an anonymous survey allows your team to share ideas on what can be better. Additionally, daily or regular interactions with your team are important, along with one-on-one meetings so you can continually keep a finger on the pulse of the organization.

CULTIVATE YOUR CULTURE

In everything we do, we want our team to know their voices are heard. Company culture is key to employee retention and engagement, and it can also impact client relationships. Because of our positive culture, our clients have built relationships with our employees. They have become accustomed to interacting with the same people year after year, and this raises the bar in the industry.

It's impossible to build rapport with your account representative if that person changes all the time. Continuity is important. I recall when one of our representatives was promoted and our clients were not happy—not because they weren't supportive of his success, but because they were comfortable working with him, and it was difficult to transition to someone new.

There's no doubt our culture has enhanced our client relationships. In some cases, it's actually helped us attract new clients. Our pitch for new business is all about our culture, our vision, and our social impact programs. There are some clients who simply want to know that we will do the work, but this novel approach has differentiated us from the other pitches.

I encourage you to chart your own course when it comes to creating lasting company culture. Don't just copy what I did. Think about the original vision you had for your own business. Think about your team, clients, and vendors, and what you want them to experience when they work with you and for you. Take feedback from both and incorporate it into your employee programs and the services you offer to clients. Cultures are built over time, and if they are cultivated properly, they can only get better.

 To learn more about leadership and its impact on company culture, check out the *#BeBetter with Michael Kurland* podcast "How Leaders Can Create a Great Place to Work" with Michael C. Bush, CEO of Great Place to Work®. Go to MichaelKurland.co/BeBetter-Podcast.

CHAPTER 8

BE PROFITABLE

Selling for Success

I'm always excited to talk about one of my favorite topics: sales.

If you think about it, you're selling something to someone every single day. You sell yourself at a job interview. You sell an idea to your boss. You sell a project to your team.

Everyone always wants to know what makes a great salesperson. There are a ton of books with amazing tips on how to close deals. Many provide step-by-step instructions and promise that commission checks will pour in. But at its foundation, sales is about people. If you don't like people, you're not going to be a successful salesperson. Solid social skills are a must-have in building lasting relationships with your clients.

A good primer for anyone who wants a career in sales is waiting tables or tending bar. These jobs help you refine your ability to talk to people you don't know and learn how to cultivate relationships. If you do it well, they'll be back. If not, well, being able to accept rejection is part of the sales process.

Likeability, passion for your product or service, and relationships are key to selling successfully. Here are some tips on how to Be Profitable and sell for success.

KNOW YOUR CLIENTS

One of the reasons I have been so successful is because I know my clients and I know them well. When I pick up the phone to call them, I ask about their family or we talk about the scores of last night's game. I put their birthdays and other important dates in my calendar so I remember to reach out to them. My clients are not commodities or simply a means to my bottom line. They are people, and the ability to connect with them on a human level is an important factor in being a successful salesperson.

Having a good memory also helps, and I have a good one for trivia. I remember the names of my clients' boyfriends, girlfriends, spouses, kids, or their favorite baseball teams. How do I know this information? Because I get to know them. It's about forming a relationship with another person that goes deeper than the product or service you are selling.

In today's challenging business climate, empathy, compassion, and vulnerability are key to lasting success. When we can put ourselves in another person's shoes—in this case, our prospect or client's shoes—we can relate to them and the challenges they are facing. The only way to do this is by getting to know them as a whole person, not just as a data point in your CRM system.

BELIEVE IN WHAT YOU SELL

Another trait of a great salesperson is that they believe in what they are selling. This is critical—you need to have a deep conviction that your product or service is the best. When you are able to effectively communicate the value to your prospects, they can trust what you say. If you're excited about what you're selling and can communicate it, you're likely to close the deal on the table and, more importantly, solidify the relationship.

For a business owner, this passion and product knowledge should be in your DNA. It's your company, so of course you should know the most about whatever it is you are offering.

For the first two and a half years of Branded Group, Kiira and I were 24/7/365 selling machines, but we knew we could not sustain the pace. We had to hire additional salespeople if we wanted to continue our growth. One of the key questions every business owner should ask in this situation is "How can I find people who will care about my business as much as I do?" Unfortunately, the reality is no one's ever going to care as much as you do, and you will have to accept that from the start. However, you will find team members who are going to rally right alongside you through thick and thin to help your business succeed. They will go above and beyond without being asked. They'll sign up for those extra projects and offer suggestions on how you can improve your products or processes.

While it's your responsibility to create a product or service you are proud to stand behind, your team also wants to believe in what they're selling. They want to know that what they're offering to clients works. When they are proud of the product, they'll look forward to selling. If your products are broken or you have less-than-optimal service, your clients are going to be upset, and your team is not going to want to sell for you.

OVERCOME YOUR FEAR OF REJECTION

When a "thanks, but no thanks" response doesn't faze you or stop you from moving forward, then you know you have the resilience and perseverance needed to be successful in sales. Everyone will face a setback, a lost client, or a botched deal, but the key is to brush yourself off and move on. I've been told no plenty of times, but I've used it to pivot the conversation, and guess what? I've walked out of the door with a yes. Maybe not every time, but enough.

This is why I'm a firm believer that every young person should spend time working in the restaurant or retail industries. The skills needed to process rejection and move on can be fine-tuned in these early stomping grounds. If you can look back at each customer interaction as a lesson to learn from, you can see what went well and what didn't. You can ask yourself, *Why did this person turn me down? What could I have done differently?* If you understand people, their motives, and their needs, you can better respond to them and provide solutions.

It's why coaches review the video of each game with their team. They examine each and every play of their own as well as those of their opponents so they can get better and do things differently next time. A successful salesperson should do the same thing after every client interaction.

Here's where your ability to accept rejection comes in. What if that potential client doesn't need your product or service?

Simple. You just say, "Thank you for your time," and move on. There will be others who will want what you're selling—I guarantee it.

The following questions can guide your postgame analysis:

- Why did client A say no? How can I change that to a yes?
- Why did client B say yes? What went well?
- Why did client C say not now? When can I follow up?

When the rejection comes, many new salespeople let fear take over. They start asking themselves, *What if I don't make my goal? Am I going to lose my job?* Do not let yourself go there. Remember, Rome wasn't built in a day, and that no on Monday could easily turn into a yes the following Wednesday.

Would you rather be a one-hit wonder or have repeated success every day?

I am not advocating for being pushy, because that's annoying and may ruin your chances of building any type of long-term relationship. When you're continually aggressive, your potential client questions your motivation. You don't care about them; you only care about the deal. They'll think you're only focused on getting one sale now rather than fostering a relationship long term. Better to be someone who can hit a single every time you're up to bat than someone who hits one home run and never scores again.

Maybe there's a new product line or simply a tweak to a service that emerges from this rejection. If you're willing to listen and to learn from each encounter, the possibilities are endless. Your priority should always be strengthening the client relationship by listening to what they have to say, as well as listening to what your sales team is sharing with you. Feedback is critical to the growth of your company, whether it comes from your clients, your colleagues, or even your competitors. Never dismiss it. Listen to the good and the bad because both can propel you in new directions.

MENTOR YOUR SALES TEAM

Some people can sell anything and don't necessarily care about the quality of the product or service. It's just a job to them. Other people have to care about the product before they'll ever reach out to a single client. In your hiring interviews, you will have to determine which type of person each candidate is. Do you want brand champions who are in it for the long term or robots who can sell? Only you can decide.

As I said, no one is going to believe in your company and its offerings as much as you. However, you can and should be hiring fellow cheerleaders. Your sales team is going to need training in order to be able to speak confidently about your business, as well as know how to approach your clients in a professional manner. Most companies have a sales training period, and new hires are given materials and demonstrations to strengthen their knowledge. But how can a new business owner accomplish this when these resources are unavailable? You will have to get creative.

I took my newly hired sales team on the road with me. I watched how they conducted themselves with our clients. I supervised their phone calls. I'm sure it was uncomfortable for them, but

I needed to see how they were representing my company. I also wanted to be able to help them.

In this way, I served as their mentor: I openly and regularly shared best practices with them so they would learn how to build relationships with our clients. I spoke to them about the importance of listening to understand, rather than listening to respond.

Your sales team should do a fair amount of homework to learn about their clients' needs. Some of this background information is done passively, like checking out their websites. But the other part is by listening—*really listening*. Your salespeople need to be excellent listeners; otherwise, they're going to waste their time and your potential client's time trying to jam a square peg into a round hole, selling them something they don't want or need.

HAVE MEANINGFUL CONVERSATIONS

Meaningful conversations with your clients can turn your business in a brand-new direction—if you're open to it.

Listening to both team members and clients has led us to expand our business in ways we never anticipated. Years ago, we hired a graphics installation team member. She had many connections with companies offering this service and asked if we wanted to get into that line of business. We knew it was a risk, but we took that conversation seriously and opted to pursue a new niche for us. Turns out, we tapped into a service our clients really valued, and now it's an additional revenue stream. Listening paid off.

Another example: years ago, we were asked if we provided

maintenance for kitchen equipment or if we handled janitorial services. We didn't at that time, but the person who was asking was a loyal client, and we wanted to help them. So we invested time to research a solution, and now we also offer this service.

Other times, meaningful conversations can be a little more difficult. We once were asked to do milkshake-machine repairs for a restaurant client. No matter how we tried, we just couldn't get it right.

Here's a key lesson. While we did our best to fulfill the request, when we realized it was not our strength, we had to decide if we were going to invest more resources into figuring it out or walk away. Sure, we could've thrown more money at the problem, but was that in our best interest? Was it in the best interest of the client? Ultimately, we decided to preserve the relationship by having the tough conversation. We admitted we were not a good fit and recommended they find an alternative solution. You know what? They appreciated the honesty. Now we have an even better relationship.

This can be a difficult decision, especially when you first launch your company. Turning away business while you are trying to grow can be painful. However, it is sometimes necessary for the long-term health of your business.

BE SELECTIVE

As a new entrepreneur, you may not have the luxury of saying no to clients. Beggars can't always be choosers. But over time, it is important to know what type of clients you want and know their ROI. Otherwise, you're risking your financial health and potentially damaging your reputation, as unhappy clients will have no problem telling others of their less-than-stellar experience with your company.

It is important to understand the dollars and cents behind every sale. For example, in my past sales roles, I would take any deal I could get to achieve my goals. But just because we made revenue didn't mean it was a good deal. It might look like a $50,000 bump in the monthly budget, but how much is that client costing you? If they're not a match, you may be spending more time and money managing them.

For example, we once had a client who would challenge us on every invoice, every work order, and every proposal. So, while the bottom line looked like it was increasing, our expenses to manage them were as well. We were making pennies, and we had to deal with the continual headaches.

Interestingly, our contact left, and their replacement was friendly and welcoming. Had we damaged the relationship because the client wasn't profitable, the new contact may have fired us. Sometimes, the person on the other end of the phone simply wants to win. They want to look good in front of their boss. They want to make their numbers, just as you do. But when their continual pushback results in wasted time and negatively impacts your bottom line and your team's productivity and morale, you will have to decide whether or not they are worth retaining. The sooner you identify and deal with these types of clients, the better.

If you're spending more time and resources on a client who is barely giving you any business or is actually costing you money, it may be time to cut the cord. Yet, whenever possible, always strive to preserve the relationship. Even though you've lost the client's business, they will remember your professionalism.

SELL WITH INTEGRITY

Always be authentic in all of your personal and professional dealings. *Always*.

As a CEO, you are the face of your organization. Your reputation is critical, and I mean critical. You're the brand. I never take any risks that might tarnish my reputation. Additionally, I have a team that needs me to lead by example. Your integrity and character are front and center, so doing what you say and saying what you mean are how you have to show up to the world.

I've never been anyone but myself to secure a sale, which is what differentiates me from a lot of other people. What you see is what you get.

Part of building relationships is establishing trust from the very first encounter. When you continuously do what you say you will do, your trustworthiness deepens and clients or employees will be able to count on you. Additionally, if you make a mistake, own up to it immediately. Then, do all you can to fix the problem. Honesty is always the best policy.

KEEP THE BIG PICTURE IN MIND

Because we were focused on building relationships, not simply selling our services, I knew our clients would value this approach and continue to support our growing business. I also knew that relationship-building took time and effort, but if I or my team wanted to be perceived positively, we would have to be committed to knowing our clients better than anyone else. We would have to be proactive, responsive, and efficient in all of our dealings with them. We'd have to Be Better.

Today, our clients describe us as caring, honest, and authentic. They have provided priceless testimonials about our outstanding communication and BeBetter Experience. Our core values reflect these traits, which make the difference between simply being a salesperson and being a customer relationship expert.

We often hear the term "it factor" on TV competitions when judges are seeking someone who has more than talent, who has the potential to be a star. The same applies for your sales team. You can teach anyone your processes and procedures, but if they aren't inherently motivated to sell, it's going to be a challenge.

Another salesperson was a different story initially. At first, he just wanted to make money, which was fine, but it couldn't be the sole motivator for his success. I spent a fair amount of time teaching him how to improve. As I began to know him better, I saw his individual strengths and skills. This was important because I didn't want a team of robots. I wanted relationship builders. Today, he is an outstanding salesperson.

Money and big commission checks can be encouraging at first, but you have to keep the big picture in mind. If your salespeople are only in it for the money, eventually they are going to burn out. If they know the value your products or services are bringing to your clients, it changes their mindset and creates a more sustainable approach to sales.

At the writing of this book, I was in the process of hiring another salesperson. My existing sales team consisted of four people who were laser focused on bringing in new clients. They had a clear process and were motivated but had few contacts in the industry, given that they were relatively new. I was seeking someone who could bring their connections who also had a big-picture mindset and a selfless "when one of us wins, we all win" mentality. I needed someone who understood that if one person gets the lead but another closes the deal, it's fine. We all win.

Healthy competition is good, but if it causes discord within your team because everyone is fighting for the same commission check, it's time to reevaluate. That's a short-term sales strategy, and again, it's not sustainable because either your sales team is going to burn out or your clients are going to pick up on this negative vibe and run.

BUILD A DIVERSE SALES TEAM

Diversity is a key component of your team's creativity.

It may be tempting to hire clones of yourself, but building a sales team is like putting a puzzle together. If all of the pieces are the same, you'll never be able to complete it. Similarly, in a sales team, or any team for that matter, its members have to be different.

One person may shy away from cold calling and lean toward virtual conversations. Another may be a people person, but technology is a challenge. One may be afraid of rejection, and another embraces it. Everyone brings something different to the table, and that makes for a solid team.

You need to have a variety of people and personalities. Your star salesperson may rub a client the wrong way, but someone else on your team may be a perfect fit. Each has their strengths and weaknesses, but every member of the team has to have an inviting personality and inherently like talking to people.

You don't have to be an extrovert, but you have to be able to engage with people. You need to interact with them, be a good listener, and foster the relationship. This is the human side of sales. There is a lot of technology that can help you, but it doesn't take the place of the human touch. Complex CRM systems can assist with tracking communications, important dates, and follow-up activities—and with making sure that things aren't falling through the cracks. But at the end of the day, the most sophisticated technology can't take the place of a one-on-one conversation between your salesperson and a valued client.

The point here is that everyone is going to build their clientele differently, using their skills, personality traits, and training. Each salesperson will have or will develop a personal sales style. It's actually what differentiates them from the competition. This uniqueness should be celebrated and strengthened.

Of course, that doesn't mean you let your team go rogue! This is where solid training in your company's sales processes comes into play. Ultimately, if your sales team exhibits authenticity and is trustworthy, your clients are going to respond positively and want to work with you.

BE FLEXIBLE

As a business owner, you will need to be open-minded about the "how" of achieving your sales targets. If sales goals are clear and you have a motivated team, it makes no difference if they connect to your clients via phone, LinkedIn message, or text. When people have the freedom and authority to act and do things their way, the possibilities are endless.

Sometimes, you might have to go against what's usually done or expected.

Years ago, we were asked to pitch a new account. This took place at a large symposium, and there were many other companies that wanted to land the client. We were invited to the table because of our relationship with one of the subsidiaries of the parent company. To win this account would be huge. We had 30 minutes.

As expected, the other companies spoke about their KPIs, the dollars and cents, and the services they offered. My salesperson and I took a different approach. Instead of talking about the various facility management services we offered, we spoke about our social impact program. We talked about how many houses our team had built for Habitat for Humanity of Orange County. We shared how many hours we volunteered doing beach cleanups and food drives. We spoke about our culture and our vision.

After the meeting, the two representatives told us how much they loved everything we presented. They related to our giveback initiatives and how we cared for our employees. They noted how they aligned with our vision and that they wanted to work with us. Today, they are one of our top five clients because we "sold" them on *why* we do what we do, not the *what*.

To this day, I'm most proud of this sale because we showcased who we were as an organization. Our willingness to be flexible and change up the way we pitched our business led to a successful relationship with a client who fully supported our vision.

I could've taken the traditional route and told them how we do facility management better or that our turnaround time is quicker. I could've talked KPIs until I was blue in the face, but then it would've become a numbers game. As soon as I'm unable to meet your expectations, you'll go shopping for another provider. However, because clients align and support our vision, they will think twice before they move on to someone else.

Branded Group is one of many facility management providers. We offer services similar to our competition. However, what differentiates us is our commitment to Be Better. Our "why" is the foundation of every sales pitch and the reason that our valued clients trust and continue to support us.

RESPECT PEOPLE

One of the things that's made me successful in sales is my ability to read people. I think it's a sixth sense, actually. I've had this skill my entire life. I just didn't know I had it until I began my sales career. This ability to understand what is important to people is how I have built all of my client relationships. Once I tapped into this trait, I was able to take my sales skills to the next level.

I don't try to sell "things." I want you to buy my services because you like doing business with me. People want to do business with people they like. Zig Ziglar said, "If people like you, they'll listen to you, but if they trust you, they'll do business with you." Likeability. Integrity. Trustworthiness. Each of these traits has to come through, whether you're pitching a multimillion-dollar account or servicing a client request.

So, what can I do to interest you in doing business with me? The first thing is to build an authentic relationship, based on mutual respect and honesty. This goes back to what I said earlier about knowing yourself, your skills, and your talents. You need an honest assessment of what you can and cannot do.

Early in my career, I landed a major client. My boss was called to meet with them. I had moved out of the day-to-day account management because the account had grown so much. As a salesperson for a small company, my job was to sell. When my manager asked the client why they chose to work with the company, they told my manager it was because of my trustworthiness, honesty, and authenticity. When I heard this, I took it to heart. It's who I am. It's how I sell to this day.

However, even the best salesperson is going to get rejected at some point. How you handle that rejection will determine your next steps. If you fear the rejection, you'll never call on that prospect (or perhaps any others) again. If it empowers you, you'll consider a different strategy. Polite and professional follow up can be the deciding factor on whether that client will work with you in the future.

You earn people's respect by respecting them. For example, if a potential client is simply not interested, I will respect that and not bother them again. I'm not going to continue to follow up and risk annoying them to the point of them never doing business with me. However, if they leave the door open and it's simply timing, I'll ask them when to follow up. Being able to successfully pivot illustrates your self-confidence, as well as your confidence in what you are selling. If the client tells you to follow up in three months, then do it. If they say, "This product or service is not for me," respect their position and move on.

Eventually, through word of mouth, prospects will contact you. If you do your job right by treating existing and potential clients honestly and respectfully, it's going to pay off. People will begin to recommend you—even those prospects who turned you down, if you didn't burn a bridge. Your services may not have been right for them, but they may be right for someone they know. This is why it's so important to foster good relationships.

MANAGE YOUR TIME

Another trait of a good salesperson is time management. Effectively and efficiently managing time makes you more productive and decreases stress because you know exactly how your day is planned. Setting aside time to make calls, mine your database or LinkedIn contacts, and follow up thoughtfully is much easier when you singularly focus on each of these tasks for a specific period of time. Doing a little of this and a little of that with no focus can lead to mixed results.

When you first launch your business and are trying to secure clients, it may be difficult to have an organized approach to time management. In those early days, you're hungry and you have to be able to crush the phones, emails, or whatever channel you're using to contact your prospects. Eventually, this frantic pace subsides as you hire a team to assist you and regular business begins to filter in.

Today, I rely on my sales team, who are second to none in this industry. I only speak with clients if someone asks for me. They trust that our sales team can handle whatever their needs are and that they will always deliver upon our promise to Be Better.

STAY CONNECTED

In my early days in sales, there were no fancy CRM applications. In fact, email was just taking off. I'm really dating myself now! Back then, the way to make a sale was to pound the phones, dial for dollars, as they say. My goal every day was to make 100 calls. Because I made a commission on every sale, my motivation was to call as many people as possible. I was selling industrial equipment, and this was a big-ticket item. If I could sell just one each day, that was considered a good week. More than five made for a great week.

I also made money on the consumables, such as machine parts and accessories. Those could easily be sold every day, but I still had to work the phones. I had to learn how to strengthen relationships so the people on the other end would take my calls and listen to my sales pitch. Even though email took over and was the preferred method of communication, the "rules" of selling didn't change.

Today, LinkedIn and other social media platforms are popular. Instead of face-to-face meetings, Zoom calls are scheduled.

Many of our connections are virtual. But while you may have to use new methods for selling, the basics never change. Relationships must still be created and developed. Trust must be established.

Whether you're sitting in a restaurant closing a deal or texting on WhatsApp, without trust, transparency, and authenticity, the deal will not be made.

My preferred method of communication is still face-to-face or over the phone, but I had to adjust as the culture and technology evolved. People don't always answer their phones. With spam and telemarketing calls flooding our voicemails, most people ignore incoming calls from numbers they don't recognize. Emails used to be cool, but now with automated-drip marketing campaigns filling our inboxes, even they are getting ignored. Knowing how to rise above the noise is critical.

Utilizing any and all means available to you so you can connect with your clients is the mark of a solid salesperson. Once the connection is made, the relationship can begin. There's no one way to do this anymore. Some people will answer their phone. Some will respond to that cool marketing campaign. Still others will want to meet you in person. When you know your client well, you will know their preferred method of communication and utilize it in your interactions.

What I'm about to say next is going to sound very old school: don't underestimate the power of a handwritten note. Again, you have to rise above the noise. So, be creative! When was the last time you received a letter in the mail? How did you feel? I suspect you were a little excited. I bet it captured your attention. My father used to send me handwritten letters once or twice each month. I can't tell you how much those meant to me. Consider this option for your next client outreach.

Today's CRM systems make it easy to stay on top of your leads, their communication preferences, and important dates like birthdays or anniversaries. Review this information periodically, so you can weed out those contacts who are not interested or not worth pursuing. We all want to have a healthy prospects database, so remember: garbage in, garbage out.

People move around frequently these days. No one stays at a job for 30 years anymore. Yesterday, Maria was your contact at Acme, Inc. Today, it's Leonard. Tomorrow, it'll be someone else. Lead mining or prospecting is likely the most underrated activity in sales. You have to do your own research to stay on top of your leads, because eventually, they will become obsolete.

For example, let's say you call on a prospect and find out that person is no longer with the company. Your immediate next step is to find out who the new person is and open the door for a conversation. Digital platforms like LinkedIn make it easy to see who's who, but never underestimate the power of personal outreach.

Moving beyond the word "client" or "customer" to a term like "partner" is the end goal. Partners are there for the long haul. They are there during the uncertainties of your business (or theirs). I'm grateful for the trusted partnerships we've built at Branded Group. Our clients and vendors know we are who we say we are. We will do what we say we will do. That's trust.

KNOW WHO YOU ARE

Building trust takes time; however, being patient with yourself, your team, and the process is key to withstanding the roller coaster of sales. As a salesperson, knowing who you are and what your skills and talents are also helps you to know your best role within the sales process.

For example, some salespeople are "hunters." These are the people who go out and get the new business and get the prospect excited about the service or product. Then, there's the person who closes the deal. They've mastered all the details of the operational procedures and can get the new client onboarded. Next, there's the person who will deepen the relationship day to day.

Every part of the process is important. If you are just starting out in sales, I encourage you to work in an organization where you can learn the entire process. Then, when you get to a bigger organization, you will be able to function well in any of these roles.

Today on my team, I have people who are strong hunters and others who are customer solution managers, handling the day-to-day operations of managing the account and being the client voice inside our organization. You need both. Remember, it's easier to keep a client than to get a new one, so having a strong inside salesperson who can revive stagnant accounts can make all the difference.

Lastly, your sales team has to trust you, their CEO. They have to trust that you will pay their commission, that you will coach them out of difficult situations, and that they can come to you with ideas, challenges, and more. Follow through on your commitments. Don't be an adversary. Work together. You're all on the same team with the same goal: to grow the business.

 To learn more about how to spark inspiration in your culture, check out the *#BeBetter with Michael Kurland* podcast "How Company Culture Drives Exceptional Customer Service" with Dale Moore, Head of Service at Hope Builders, Inc. Go to MichaelKurland.co/BeBetter-Podcast.

CHAPTER 9

BE SERVICE-ORIENTED

Creating the Client Experience

I grew up in lower Fairfield County, Connecticut, which is the home of Stew Leonard's, an amazing business that started out as a small dairy store in the late 1960s. Today, it is known as the "World's Largest Dairy Store" but more so as one of the most renowned grocery stores in the country. They earned this designation because of a few words that are painted on a huge rock that greets each customer as they enter the store:

Rule 1: The customer is always right!

Rule 2: If the customer is ever wrong, reread Rule 1!

Ensuring that your customers or clients have a memorable, personalized, and enjoyable experience is an important differentiator, whether you are an e-commerce or traditional brick-and-mortar business.

As a facility management company, it's our job to preserve brand standards. If we don't do that, our clients will find someone who does. It's that simple. The facility management industry is all about service. We don't sell products, so we are only as good as the services we provide.

From day one, our goal at Branded Group was to Be Better, and that includes how we treat our clients, subcontractors, team, and anyone who supports us. Creating a positive client experience starts with being service-oriented to everyone.

Here are some practical tips on how to Be Service-Oriented and create a memorable client experience.

TAKE CARE OF YOUR EMPLOYEES FIRST

Our sales and customer service teams are the face of our company. Every day, they handle the complicated and time-sensitive needs of our clients all around the country. If we want them to treat our clients well, we must treat them well.

Taking care of our employees and helping them to Be Better is embedded within our culture. Richard Branson, founder of the Virgin Group, said it best: "Clients do not come first. Employees come first. If you take care of your employees, they will take care of the clients."

If your employees are miserable, then guess what? Your clients will be too. But if your team feels valued, appreciated, safe, and trusted, your clients are going to benefit.

One of the things we hear a lot from our clients is how they like having a dedicated account manager. They like knowing every time they pick up the phone or send an email, they're going to speak to the same person. Their call is not going to people in a huge customer service center who have no idea who they are, what they need, or how to help them. This saves them time and money because they don't have to continually retrain a new person on their facility needs. Additionally, because of our high retention rate, our clients are assured that the person they are talking to today will likely be the same person they talk to tomorrow.

Going above and beyond to deliver excellent service is what will sustain your business. Having a strategic approach to how you will deliver upon this promise has to be rooted in your culture. For example, we couldn't have a culture of being better and fail at servicing our clients. It doesn't match up. This is why we put so much time and effort into our culture and ensuring that our employees are happy. It's not just words on a wall. Again, happy employees make for happy clients.

BUILD TRUSTING RELATIONSHIPS

The essence of great customer service is when customers trust you implicitly with their business.

When asked why I think people choose us, I always have the same response: people do business with people they trust. It's simple. Our clients like us. They enjoy the relationships they have built with our team, knowing that we are dedicated to their success. Yes, we can do things more efficiently and effectively because of the fine-tuning we've done to our operations, but we have proven to our clients and vendors that they can trust us to deliver what we say we will.

"Comfort" isn't necessarily a word you think of when it comes to facility management, but it's exactly what we provide our clients and what keeps them doing business with us. Our clients are comfortable calling us any time of day or night when their facility is in trouble. Whether it's an HVAC system that went south on a hot summer day or a security system that needs an overhaul, they can pick up the phone and know they're going to get an answer. This security leads to a confidence in our ability to service their needs. They know we have their backs, and as our purpose states, we "preserve their brand standards."

IDENTIFY YOUR IDEAL CLIENT

When you're just starting out, your entire focus is on getting new business. Your sales funnel has to be continually replenished. In the beginning, you may not be able to choose your clients, and sometimes, there may be one or two that are difficult.

In the early days of Branded Group, we had our fair share of challenging clients. While we worked through them, we used that time to identify our ideal client. Let's be honest: it's easy to give great service to great customers. We knew that, to be successful, we had to identify the best recipients for our services, and we had to deliver consistent, repeatable, and memorable experiences to them.

Once the word got out about how well we treated our clients, the floodgates began to open. Referrals came in. So, while you always want to be working the sales funnel, you also must be continually refining your customer service operations. There's nothing better than a heartfelt testimonial or Google review to create repeat business and secure new clients.

As your business matures and sales begin to pick up, you may want to consider reviewing your CRM database to identify if your existing clients align with your revenue or business goals, as well as your company's core values. I remember having to let go of a few clients over the years who no longer met these criteria. While you may not be able to do this yet, it is important to ensure that your clients are on board with the vision of your organization. If not, this lack of alignment may take a toll on your bottom line, negatively affect employee morale, and also impact you as the CEO because your team is not going to feel supported if you allow them to be treated poorly.

The good news is challenging situations can open the door for an honest discussion with your clients about what's working and what isn't in the business relationship. If the "broken-ness" is on your side, try to fix it to the best of your ability. If you can't, it may be time to sever the relationship. Sometimes, these conversations can lead to major process improvements that will benefit all of your clients, so it's important to be open-minded and humble. But if it becomes a case of a client "nickel and diming" your business, the effort may not be worth it.

IMPROVE YOUR CUSTOMER SERVICE

You can't fix what you don't measure.

How do you know if you're delivering excellent service? Having happy clients is one metric. Repeat business may be another. Yet, asking your clients what they like and don't like with a survey can help you to identify holes in your processes and ways you can improve.

We conduct surveys with our clients and subcontractors because we want to always be improving. If we don't have competent service providers, we'll have dissatisfied clients. Likewise, if we have difficult clients, our subcontractors aren't happy. Lastly, if our team is not delivering top-notch service, then nobody wins.

We have implemented a rating system that our customer service team uses for our subcontractors and vice versa. This 360-degree feedback enables us to continually refine our processes. These metrics are important because they help us to gauge which subcontractors are providing excellent service. Great service is not just for our clients but for our subcontractors too, as they are an extension of our brand. Those who are delivering on our promise to Be Better are rewarded with more work. If they fail to honor their commitments, we won't work with them again.

Our Preferred Vendor Program was born out of this rating system. As each vendor proved over time that they could deliver high-quality work, they were rewarded with this designation. You have to find ways to recognize the people who are helping grow your business. Whether it's your employees, your vendors, or even your clients, each is an important part of your success.

BE HONEST

Honesty is a key element of customer service.

I learned early on that if I or anyone on my team was going to promise something to a client, we had to deliver on it. Your integrity and character are part of your brand. If you have to be dishonest in order to secure a client, it's going to come back to you. We are always transparent in our business dealings because it builds trust, and as I've stated repeatedly, trust builds relationships. Whether you know it or not, you're in the business of building relationships, no matter if you're selling a product or performing a service.

We've had many clients who have called on us because they had a bad experience elsewhere. Some of these requests resulted in a one-time job. However, many of them turned into long-term relationships. I believe it's because we are honest and reliable.

INTEGRATE OPERATIONAL PROCESSES AND TECHNOLOGY

Another element of customer service is ensuring that your operational processes are integrated. This function must go hand in hand with honesty. For example, if your sales team is promising something your back office can't support, the client is going to suffer. Sales and customer service must be in lockstep so no one is overpromising and underdelivering. Again, this builds trust with the client and also builds trust in your teams, which is important.

There must be a level of trust among your employees so everyone feels valued and appreciated for what they bring to the table. For example, your sales team is working hard to secure new clients. When they close a deal, they're in the limelight and get all of the attention. However, the back-office staff is key to onboarding and the daily servicing of the client, and the accounting and vendor relations teams are a vital part of the client experience. Everyone is needed, and each team must appreciate and respect the contributions of their teammates.

Football games are not won by the quarterback but by every player.

It's also important for each department to connect and communicate on a regular basis so there are no surprises. For example, if the sales team has a goal of landing 10 new clients, but the back-office staff isn't prepared, no one will achieve their goals. Clients will be unhappy, and your team will be frustrated.

In addition to fine-tuning operational processes and ensuring your customer service team is engaged, technology can help improve your service. I mentioned earlier about how Jon Thomas was key in the overhaul of nearly every process, procedure, and system when he arrived. Because of his efforts, we have the capability to record metrics (KPIs) that enable us to analyze our service and improve upon it.

For example, analyzing our call volume tells us a story about the client. If they regularly contact us once per week and we notice a decline, this should trigger a phone call to find out what's going on. If a client is only calling us for emergencies or we see it's taking twice as long to complete a job, it's time to get on the phone with them. This is where having a solid CRM system, as well as comprehensive management reports, can help you to identify the root causes of issues. If you're not regularly analyzing your sales data, you may be missing opportunities to improve.

Complacency is to be avoided at all costs. Whether your bottom line is booming or suffering, never discount the importance of reviewing the numbers. We have a solid foundation of data analytics that are reviewed continuously, and we're always learning about new and better ways to be more efficient.

Today, our data analytics are more sophisticated than when we launched. What I needed in our first days to keep our clients happy is very different from what I need today. In the early stages, I only needed to know how we could make money, get new clients, and close jobs. Today, this information is still important, but now we are able to mine our data and implement or adjust processes as needed. There's always something to learn from analyzing your metrics.

PROBLEM-SOLVERS GET CALLED FIRST

Every industry is going to have a different approach to customer service, yet everyone has the same goal: repeat business. It's much easier to keep a customer than to get a new one. Just take a look at acquisition costs versus retention costs. Every person working in customer service should have the goal of creating repeat business.

I'm always happy to give my own business to people who have served me well in the past. Several years ago, I was in the market for a new car and I emailed a person I had dealt with previously. Even though I knew he did not sell the make and model I was looking to buy, I was happy working with him and wanted to give him the opportunity because of how well he'd treated me. I called him first.

Isn't that what we all want our clients to do? Don't we always want them to call and offer us the opportunity first? Even if you can't help them, you may be able to direct them to someone who can. Even though I did not purchase my car from that salesperson, he was helpful to the process.

Great customer service is about solving someone else's problems, creating loyal customer relationships, and setting the foundation for repeat business.

When you can do all three better than someone else, it will keep your sales funnel full and your company growing. Invest in your customer service, invest in your team, and invest in your processes and data analytics. These will pay off with a healthy bottom line and, more importantly, happy clients and employees.

 To learn more about how leaders can promote a continuous learning culture, check out the *#BeBetter with Michael Kurland* podcast, "Be Better by Being Humble" with Tarell Hannah, Sr. Facilities Manager of Shake Shack. Go to MichaelKurland.co/BeBetter-Podcast.

CHAPTER 10

BE EFFICIENT

Scaling for Sustainable Growth

CONTRIBUTORS: KIIRA BELONZI AND JON THOMAS

When Branded Group was launched, Kiira and I worked together on the operations. There was not a lot of structure, especially in those first few months. I was out pounding the pavement to get clients, and Kiira was, as she would say, acting as a "glorified coordinator." Between the two of us, we ran the service orders and established the foundation for the customer service function.

We were running a lean operation. The "keep it simple" approach was critical. Kiira did most of the operations, and I helped out when she needed a break or the volume increased. In those first days, we did things like assemble desks and set up computers. We had to be able to answer calls and conduct many of the tasks we took for granted in our corporate jobs, like IT or accounting. We were not experts in these areas, but we were determined to figure it out. We had to. And so will you.

You may be able to piecemeal these processes in the early days of your business, making it up as you go along. However, in order to scale for future growth, you need to be efficient. You need a comprehensive operations function that is continuously evaluated, so you are delivering top-notch service to your clients, as well as enabling your team to work seamlessly and avoid duplication of efforts.

Here are some practical tips on how you can Be Efficient and scale your business for future growth.

START WITH WHAT YOU KNOW

When launching a business, there is much you will not know, and it can be overwhelming. Instead of trying to learn everything, tap into the knowledge, tools, and processes you already know.

We used our operational expertise and the lessons we learned from our previous jobs to create simple processes to get our clients up and running as quickly as possible. There is always going to be a better, faster way to get things done. Humble beginnings, right? For example, we installed a CRM software package that we used in our previous company because we were familiar with it. Starting with where you are at and with what you know can save you time and money.

BE DETAIL ORIENTED

For the first six months, I was doing billing several hours each week in addition to sales. We were also doing emergency work on the weekends, so we were never getting any time off for ourselves. It was getting more and more challenging for me to have time to meet with potential clients. We knew we needed to begin hiring people to handle some of these tasks.

We opted to hire someone to help us with the accounting and billing. This seemed like a simple process: put an ad on the internet, interview people, and hire them.

However, Kiira and I learned the hiring process was far from simple. She had to become familiar with California employment law. She had to make sure she was setting up our files properly and securing the documentation needed by the state. She had to set up a timekeeping system to track sick time and other paid time off. We both had to learn what we could and could not ask in the interview process. Kiira had to know which files could be electronic and which had to be paper. We assumed everything could be electronic, only to find out later this wasn't the case. With each new hire, we learned something. For example, when one of our employees didn't show up for work, we realized we didn't have their emergency contact information.

When you launch a business, these are the details you have to consider. If you're leaving a corporate job to become an entrepreneur, you can't take their sophisticated systems with you, nor is it likely you can purchase them on day one. It may be a bit rocky at first, and the learning curve may be steep.

ESTABLISH PROCEDURES

Scaling your business is a rinse-and-repeat process. But this continuous improvement process can be fun if it's done when your hair is not on fire.

Establishing procedures and setting up a structure for your company is much easier if it's done before you actually need them. For example, if you know you're eventually going to hire people, consider drafting new-hire checklists, researching employment law, or writing those "how-to" guides. Make sure that they are scalable and will work whether you have two employees or 2,000.

Kiira actually wrote our first employee handbook. From Google searches of existing handbooks and best practices, she was able to put together the "rules" of being a Branded Group employee. To assist us with the legalities and intricacies of hiring, we contracted a human resources consultant. She was able to help us onboard our new team members, ensuring that we were adhering to state regulations and securing all of the necessary paperwork required. These laws change depending on the size of your team, and we learned that having a handful of employees is very different from having 50.

This is when your mentor as well as your professional network can be invaluable. First, an experienced mentor can guide you on who to hire, or at least who to reach out to. Attorneys, CPAs, HR managers, and operational experts can and should be in your "back pocket." You will need these people to get your business off the ground and to grow the team that's going to move you past the startup phase to being a full-fledged business.

We continued to bring on people and provided them with high-level training. Ideally, we would've preferred to have them immersed in a week of training on our processes and procedures, but we needed them to hit the ground running. Kiira provided basic instruction to our new hires, and they shadowed her on how to run work orders. It was very much a "learn-as-you-go" approach. With each new service call, we refined our processes so that when formal procedures were written, they would reflect the "nitty-gritty" of each client interaction.

NEVER LET 'EM SEE YOU SWEAT

Kiira continued to run the operations function, but as we grew, this was getting more and more difficult. She was over capacity and working nonstop answering emergency service calls in the middle of the night. She was living and breathing Branded Group. Since our team members were still relatively new, delegating was challenging.

It is tempting to think that your operational processes and procedures have nothing to do with your company culture, but they do. Things like payroll running smoothly, computers working properly, and emails being delivered are all a part of how your team functions. When you align your people and your purpose with profit, you create a solid company culture.

Yet, despite the "chaos" behind the scenes Kiira and I were experiencing, our clients never knew about it. Because of Kiira's dedication, our customer service was impeccable. Kiira made sure our clients were getting exactly what we promised, despite having a team that was "green behind the ears."

It's important to know when you've hit capacity and are maxed out. Ideally, you don't want to get to this point and hire people out of desperation, so be sure to keep a pulse on yourself, your team, and the increasing workload.

To address the increasing volume of service calls, we hired a full-time vice president of operations. She had solid industry experience and was able to take all these day-to-day tasks off of Kiira's plate. In those early days, Kiira and I could piece some processes together, but as she would say, "It was time to be a real company. It was time to stop playing small business owner and actually be one." With our sales, operations, and customer service functions in place, in order to continue our growth, we recognized the need to become more efficient and streamline processes.

Enter our President and operational guru, Jon Thomas. Jon describes himself as a change agent and proudly displays the title of "nerd." He excels in organizational structure and analytics. Jon and his team have revolutionized our internal processes through technology, solid business intelligence, and an immovable commitment to Be Better. They leave no stone unturned, and because of their expertise, Branded Group has experienced tremendous year-over-year growth and increased client retention. We've also seen improved engagement of our team, who welcome his dedication to making their jobs easier.

EVOLVE

The "fundamentals" of any high-volume operation are rooted in repetition.

From the very first day, Kiira and I knew we could transform Branded Group into a multimillion-dollar organization. We had the drive, the experience, and the dedication, but neither of us would be able to reach this kind of growth without solid, repeatable structures and processes. This is what Jon brought and continues to bring to the table. He's a big-picture thinker, and we knew he could get us there. We tapped into his operational expertise as we were launching the company, and he helped us with our initial procedures and systems.

When Jon came on board, he tore apart every single process we had and started over. He organized our workflows, and he systemized the repetitive processes so that we could be more efficient. It was painful at first, but it was necessary. Jon is all about the nuts and bolts of business—the "non-fluffy" things that are in the back of the house but make the front of the house shine.

He developed new procedures, and Kiira socialized them with the staff. This is a good example of tapping into your team's strengths. While I'm sure it was difficult for Kiira to watch Jon refine her processes, she was open-minded and humble enough to realize that, if we were to grow, our company's operations needed an overhaul. She was then able to use her strengths and talents in hiring and training to ensure our team members had the skills needed to be successful. Today, she excels at leading all of our employee-development and leadership-training efforts.

Never put a process on a pedestal. Never be married to one particular way of doing things. If you want to scale anything, no matter how small you think the business is or how simple you think it is, you need a solid foundation, and that foundation is rooted in your processes. If you think, *Oh, I've put a few processes in place. I'm done*, you're wrong.

You have to be ready to rip apart anything and everything you set up. If you are not evolving, you are dying. Jon shares this mentality, and it's what has driven our uber-efficient processes.

DELEGATE AND LET GO

Every small business owner needs to learn to let go and trust their team to do what they do best. This isn't limited to letting go of tasks—you'll also have to let go of your ego and the idea that no one else can do what you do.

I am not a process guy. I'm into the vision and the strategy. My eyes glaze over when I'm given too many details. Spreadsheets? No way! But for Jon, these are in his DNA. For him, a day without spreadsheets is like a day without air. Because of Kiira's passion for operations and her ability to problem-solve on the fly, we had good processes and procedures that carried us in that first year or two. However, they would not be able to carry us as we expanded.

There was no way Kiira and I could have scaled Branded Group to the size it is today. We needed an expert to help us. If either one of us refused to delegate and hire experts, Branded Group would have closed up shop. Growth and change can be scary but are always necessary to move forward. It's easier when you're surrounded by people you trust and who share your vision.

Jon is continually looking at ways for Branded Group to Be Better from an operational perspective. He looks at the facility management industry to identify trends. He reviews work orders. He does cost/benefit analyses. He is laser focused on getting maximum production with minimal overhead so our team is efficient and effective, as well as engaged and motivated. In our first year, we could only handle a few clients, but as we've grown, we can take on more without it crushing the team or our systems.

Because I implicitly trusted Jon and his abilities, he was given the freedom to do what he does best: to put his own stamp on our operations function. Jon had worked for large corporations and was able to take what he learned and bring it to Branded Group. He set up the organizational structures that enabled us to achieve our goals, appropriately scaling as we expanded year over year.

Jon took the time to ask our team a very simple question when he arrived at Branded Group: "If I can do anything to make your life easier, what would it be?" "Fix our email!" was the battle cry from the field. Jon updated our email, and this task was the first of many game-changing activities Jon would tackle.

With a new system in place, emails began to be routed appropriately. The right people were getting the right emails, and they were being addressed quickly. Jon was not an email administrator, but he was and is a great problem solver. The bigger the problem, the better. This action started us on the path of becoming more efficient. He also migrated our email and other systems into the cloud, making it possible for us to work remotely in the future. Little did we know how invaluable this would be when the pandemic occurred.

Simple changes like this are the beginnings of scaling your business. Jon describes it as "taking big piles of things, putting them into smaller piles, and then delegating those piles to the best person." Once the team saw that he could fix their biggest challenges and how he heard their pleas for help, he earned their trust. They knew he could do it again, and that's what he did. He solved one pain point after another.

"Let go" is not one of our core values, but "Be Adaptable" and "Be Humble" are two of them. They are key to our ability to grow. Each of us, including me as CEO, has to be open to change and be humble enough to ask for help. Being an entrepreneur is a process, and along the way you will have to stretch yourself and your team.

NEVER BE SATISFIED WITH THE STATUS QUO

Jon and his team help keep the Branded Group trains running. He has developed our operational philosophy, which is "Never be satisfied with the status quo." Just when you think a process is the best it can be, it's time to break it and build it up again. This is the only way to scale a business, because processes that worked for a company of 21 people won't work for 40 people or 100, which we have surpassed.

Your business operations function always has to be evolving. Year one does not look like year three or year 23. Agility is key for longevity.

Jon's approach to process improvement begins with a simple question he asks every employee: "What's your biggest pain point?" Their answers spark his team's next "home improvement project." This is how he transformed our operations. Because of this attention to the team's "operational well-being," Jon has earned the utmost respect of the entire Be Better team. He has methodically addressed every single challenge. He listens to everyone's input, finds solutions, and implements them, quickly and efficiently.

ANALYZE YOUR TIME

The faster someone finishes a job or a service call, the faster that person can move on to the next. Completed jobs are what we're selling, but I can't tell my team to work faster without giving them the tools to do so. Technology and process improvements enable us to make decisions faster. Teaching people how to strategize and manage their workflow inherently speeds up the work.

Identifying key metrics to manage the business is another area in which Jon excels. While balance sheets and P&L's paint part of the picture, there's a lot more to it.

For a facility management company, time is money. We look at things such as:

- How many phone calls are people making?
- How long do those calls last?
- How long does it take to process a job?
- How long are people's hands on a process?
- How do you reduce the number of hands?
- How much does a job cost?
- How much time does it take to complete?
- What is the opportunity cost of one job over the other?

Looking at each leg of the process is important because every piece has a data point that can be measured and improved upon. Determining which metrics apply to your business takes time and effort, but it is well worth it.

One of the metrics key to a facility management company is time, and no one understands this more than Jon. He brought his passion and his expertise for finding ways to save time and money to the Be Better table. He often says time is the ultimate equalizer.

Analyzing how long a particular task takes is a good place to start building out your KPIs. For example, if it takes you three weeks to onboard a client and costs you $5,000, how can you simplify the process? How can you speed it up so your sales team can onboard three clients? If salesperson A is outperforming salesperson B, are there tips and tricks that need to be shared with the team so everyone is more efficient?

Because of the operational efficiencies Jon and his team have put into place, efficiency has become a competitive differentiator for us. We can do more work with less people faster than other facility management companies. Our clients are loyal to us because they know we will get the job done and at a fair price.

These operational improvements could not have happened without the expertise of Jon and his team. Hire experts. Do your homework and due diligence. Do a cost analysis on everything. Get referrals and recommendations from your trusted network before making any significant investments.

Jon is always focused on what will make everyone's life a little easier so they don't spin and waste time. He doesn't just observe what is broken in our processes; he listens to the challenges people describe, and he puts solutions into place and addresses them, one by one. His team shares his curiosity for how to make things better, faster, and more cost effective. We've seen some amazing improvements throughout our organization. Each one of his team members is empowered to break a process and come up with a solution to make it better.

Today, I am no longer married to "how" things get done because we have solid processes and programs in place. I'm more focused on getting results in the best way possible. As long as you get results, are always filling your sales pipeline, and are hitting high-level goals, the process of how you do it is not as important.

I am proud to be an old dog who has been taught new tricks. As a business owner, you must be agile. I respect my team's abilities and trust that they know what to do to get the job done. We all need to "stay in our lane," as Jon says.

The functions of sales and operations are tightly linked. You can have a great product, but if you can't get it out the door, you're out of business. On the other hand, you can have a great operational process, but if your product or service is terrible, you're also out of business. You need both to be successful. You need experts in both functions, and you need to stand ready to pivot at any given moment.

 To learn more about how to launch and scale a business, check out the *#BeBetter with Michael Kurland* podcast "How to Launch a Successful Business by Never Taking No for an Answer" with Michael and Brian Speciale, Co-Founders of Cozy Comfort Company, LLC. Go to MichaelKurland.co/BeBetter-Podcast.

CHAPTER 11

BE GENEROUS
Building a Social Impact Program

The first year for any new entrepreneur can be characterized as the "hair on fire" year. Working long hours and wearing many hats, my co-founder Kiira and I were so busy we didn't have a minute to think about anything other than securing more clients, making sure the work was getting done, and handling the operations of the business so that we could keep the lights on.

During our second year, our hair was still on fire, but things began to fall into a rhythm, and I had some time to reflect. I discovered I was feeling empty inside. I questioned why I was doing what I was doing. Yes, I was providing a service to companies who needed it, but was my ownership of a facility management company going to be my legacy?

Even though I was enjoying being able to turn a profit early on in my business, I didn't feel proud of just making money. I needed a higher purpose. I wanted to give back and make a difference. I wanted to incorporate this mindset into my company's DNA. I wanted Branded Group to be known for more than just fixing things.

A lot of research explores the "high" that you get when you volunteer. It makes you feel as good as the person you are helping. Maybe it's a little selfish to get something out of volunteering, but it's a good selfish, I think.

Being generous is about doing something to make someone's life better.

Here are some tips on how to Be Generous and build a social impact program with purpose.

FIND OR CREATE GIVING OPPORTUNITIES

Unlike other organizations I have worked for, Branded Group has a common goal. That's how our award-winning One-for-One program was developed. Every client service call ties into our social impact program designed around giving back to our designated nonprofit partners. We started with Habitat for Humanity of Orange County and volunteered our time building and restoring sustainable homes.

Today, we have partnered with Feeding America, so now every call is transformed into a meal for a person serviced by this outstanding organization. By providing an outlet for other individuals—including members of my team and our clients—to give back, we collectively make a bigger impact.

Because we built our social impact program into our business operations, every employee could immediately know that, as soon as a service call was completed, a minute of volunteering was added to the "leaderboard." Over time, this would result in a new or restored sustainable home for a family in the community. These build projects also strengthened our team's interpersonal relationships, so it was a win-win for everyone.

I recall one home build project where the father spent hours commuting to and from his job. Because of the house we helped build, his commute was reduced to 10 minutes. He was able to spend more with his family. We didn't just give them four walls; we gave them memories they will treasure forever.

My team members are proud knowing that Branded Group is involved in many giving opportunities. This pride is reflected in our annual employee engagement surveys and the feedback we get showing how our team members feel we are living our vision and making an impact in other people's lives.

Our humanitarianism also goes on the road with us. We have participated in a number of industry trade shows where there were additional opportunities to change lives through a give-back program. While we certainly wanted to use these events to draw in more clients, we also wanted to leave a mark on our fellow exhibitors, attendees, and the community.

We decided to use these industry events as a means to donate to nonprofit organizations local to the conference location. Instead of simply writing a check, we involved the event's attendees in our efforts. Whoever visited our booth had an opportunity to cast a vote for one of three local nonprofits. After the show, we selected a winner, and they received a donation. This giveback was so popular, we rolled it out to all of our trade shows.

Because of this "on the road giveback program," we've been able to support local chapters of Habitat for Humanity, animal shelters, and veterans' organizations across the country. It wasn't long before other companies at these events followed suit. They say imitation is the highest form of flattery.

ESTABLISH A NONPROFIT PARTNERSHIP

When we selected our nonprofit partners, we wanted to ensure they aligned with our core values. We also wanted to feel good about who we were helping. We chose Habitat for Humanity because I volunteered with the organization while I was in college. Since they had a local chapter in Orange County, it made it easy to build a mutually beneficial relationship. Additionally, many of their build projects were close to the office, so our team members could participate.

Again, our vision is to "build a conscious business that inspires future humanitarian leaders." We focus on aligning purpose with profit, and we want our efforts to make a difference in people's lives. When we were building our program, we wanted it to align with a larger perspective.

When we learned about the United Nations Sustainable Development Goals, we took some time to evaluate the areas where we could make the most impact. The 17 goals call for every country to do their part to address the urgent needs of our world, including ending hunger, poverty, and inequality, as well as doing our part to address climate change and preserve our environment.

We initially chose to support Goal No. 11: make cities and human settlements inclusive, safe, resilient, and sustainable, making our efforts with Habitat for Humanity a perfect fit. As our social impact program evolved, we began to partner with other organizations, such as Feeding America, which aligned with Goal No. 2: end hunger, achieve food security, and improve nutrition and promote sustainable agriculture.

In recent years, we have supported Goal No. 14: conserve and sustainably use the oceans, seas, and marine resources for sustainable development. Our team has participated in beach cleanups and hosted donation drives for organizations who are helping the environment.

Anyone can write a check to their favorite charity, but I wanted my team to be able to physically do something as part of their volunteering. Then, they could immediately see the impact they were making. The result of our giving programs has been phenomenal. There have been several heartwarming stories from my team after handing over boxes of food or filling backpacks for deserving children and families. The act of giving back resulted in immediate gratitude for what they had.

SHARE THE GIVING SPIRIT WITH YOUR CLIENTS

Because our social impact program is tied to our business operations, our clients also get to participate in our initiatives. When we tell them that their 200 calls resulted in putting 200 meals on a table for a family or giving a little kid their first bedroom in their new home, I believe they are both proud and grateful to do business with us. Additionally, when we provide corporate gifts to our clients, we utilize Gifts for Good, furthering our commitment to give back. When clients see our commitment to these causes, they want to work with us.

Our clients and vendors are an integral part of us achieving our vision to "build a conscious business to inspire future humanitarian leaders." Early in my career, my focus was on making money. That was my definition of success. However, I learned through a painful divorce and many unfulfilling jobs that money was not going to make me happy. I want Branded Group to be profitable, but I want it to do more than that—not just for myself, but for my team, our clients, and the communities in which we do business.

PARTICIPATE CONSISTENTLY

As a leader of any organization, you should want your business to make an impact in more ways than simply being listed on the stock exchange. Leaders have to care about people and inspire them to Be Better.

I didn't understand this concept in my college days, when my philanthropic efforts were simply to fulfill a fraternity requirement. However, I'm grateful for this introduction to volunteering because it changed me. Now, my team and I are changing other people's lives.

Most of the members of my team willingly participate in our giveback programs, which is why it is so important to select nonprofit partners and projects your team can rally behind. It's also critical that you, as the owner or CEO, participate alongside them. Again, put legs to your legacy. Show your team this is something that's important to you.

We support multiple organizations so if one nonprofit doesn't resonate with someone on our team, they can do something else. For example, not everyone wants to build a house, but they might want to do a beach cleanup or stuff backpacks for back-to-school drives. One of our employees led a relief effort for those impacted by Hurricane Maria in Puerto Rico. She coordinated the entire project, and it was amazing!

As a new business owner, you may think you're unable to do much when it comes to giving back. You might only be able to write a small check to a local nonprofit, and that's fine. Just start from where you are. If monies aren't there, donate your time or your skills to an organization. Everyone can find an hour in their schedule to pack up boxes of food or fill a backpack.

I encourage you to find a cause you're passionate about, where you can build a long-term relationship. Don't be discouraged if your first steps are small ones. If that first partner isn't right, it's okay to move on to another. As you hire more employees, engage them in your efforts and watch how your program evolves. When we started, our efforts were primarily in Orange County, but now with an expanding workforce, we can help people in communities all over the country. Today, we are partnered with several organizations at different times of the year so there's something for everyone.

BE OPEN TO RECOMMENDATIONS

There may be efforts your team members are passionate about or deeply involved with that can add value to your program. Whether this is done through an annual survey or informal conversations, it's important that you, as their CEO or as their manager, are open to their recommendations.

Because of our team's feedback, we've adopted families at Christmas and provided gifts for the children. We've hosted food drives at Thanksgiving. Remember, your vision can't just be words on the wall; it has to be embraced by your team.

Our social impact program helps us to retain employees, which builds trust with our clients, who give us more business. This wasn't the motivation to launch this program, but it has been one of the many added benefits. Potential employees are drawn to Branded Group because they like knowing we align purpose and profit. Current employees stay because of this commitment. Vendors like working with us because they know we're about more than the bottom line. Even in sales meetings with prospective clients, we lead with our giveback strategy. We tell them about our "why," which then sells them on what we do.

My desire to be a CEO of a purpose-driven business was inspired when I read *Conscious Capitalism* by John Mackey and Raj Sisodia. I was drawn to their intention to elevate the business community by changing the paradigm about its existence. Instead of being solely focused on profits, organizations could be purposeful, creating value for their employees, clients, and community.

It's my hope that every entrepreneur and business leader incorporates some type of giving back into their business strategy. The conscious capitalism movement is growing and evolving as more and more companies align purpose with profit. There's a balance between the two, where your efforts and your team's efforts will result in a healthy bottom line and make a difference in the world.

To learn more about how we developed our mission, vision, purpose, and core values, check out the *#BeBetter with Michael Kurland* podcast "Become a Purpose-Driven Company by Giving Back Authentically" with Jennifer Bernheim, Founder of OnPurpose PR. Go to MichaelKurland.co/BeBetter-Podcast.

CHAPTER 12

BE INSPIRING

Leading for the Future

In the early days of the COVID-19 pandemic, we had a skeleton crew who put in 70-plus hours a week. They went above and beyond day after day to make sure our company didn't go out of business. That kind of loyalty can't be measured. It's priceless. I'll always be grateful to them because of their dedication and commitment under extremely difficult circumstances.

Everyone reacts to challenges differently. Some crumble, but for others, it's an invitation to dig in. A crisis, whether personal or professional, leads you to reevaluate your situation. At least it should. Think about it: if you get a bad medical report, you take steps to improve your health. If your organization is hit with a sudden challenge, you take steps to improve your operations so you can stay in business.

If you're not continuously evolving as a leader, you become stagnant, and your team will be disengaged. Here again, as soon as you think you've perfected something, tear it up and start over again. Always seek to make it even better. This can be your processes, your products and services, or even your business model. Complacency with anything is never good. Strong leaders should always be pushing their teams to avoid complacency at all costs.

What actually makes a strong leader? Are people born to lead, or are they taught? I believe it's a combination of both. You may have a talent to be a leader, but you always have to be developing the skills you lack in your tool belt. To do so, you will need to admit you have a particular weakness and be willing to develop it. Sometimes, egos get in the way because we don't want anyone to know we're weak in a particular area. You have to get out of your own way to become a better leader.

Being an inspiring leader starts with this willingness to change. Here are some practical tips to Be Inspiring by being a better leader.

EXAMINE YOUR MOTIVATION

It's always good to understand the motivation for anything you do so that you are doing it for the right reasons. Likewise, you have to examine your motivation for wanting to lead. When I launched Branded Group, I wanted to create a profitable company and a workplace where people felt care for, valued, and appreciated.

When I interviewed Michael C. Bush, CEO of Great Place to Work, for my podcast, he said, "People's perceptions are shaped primarily by whether they feel like they're being cared for as a person." As leaders, it is our job to be on the lookout for any warning signs that people may not feel this way. This can be through comments on your employee surveys, one-on-one meetings, or a gut feeling that something just isn't right.

My capacity for empathy and compassion toward others has been expanded because of what we've gone through. Also, my commitment to my employees is stronger than ever. I am going to support my team, and I'm not going to let them down. I want to ensure they know how valuable they are to me and to Branded Group.

BE TRANSPARENT

Through the multiple employee engagement surveys we've conducted over the years, I've learned a great deal about the way my team views our culture, our programs and processes, and our leadership style. A good leader has to be open to receiving feedback—good and bad—and make the necessary corrections.

In my previous jobs, I was told over and over that I'd be getting a raise. I never got it. I think my managers were hoping I'd forget about what they promised me, but I didn't. What I remember is their lack of trustworthiness.

Don't make promises you can't keep; otherwise, you will lose your credibility. One of the things we've improved upon greatly over the years is being transparent in our communications and following through on what we say. Your team can see right through you, so it's important to be authentic and truthful.

Our survey repeatedly shows that our company culture is what people enjoy and value the most about working here.

In a Town Hall meeting we had in early 2021, my team put together a video where they shared what they liked most about Branded Group. During the video, the Zoom chat was overflowing with positive comments. I'm not ashamed to say it brought a tear to my eye. See what I mean about the benefits of being transparent?

BE RESILIENT

Resiliency is also a skill good leaders need to demonstrate. I've been knocked down a lot in my life, but I've gotten back up again, and it has improved my ability to persevere through challenges and be an even better leader. Sometimes, we don't find out how strong we are until we are pushed. It's all a part of being in that mode of continuous improvement and being agile, which again, is a mindset all leaders need to have.

Agility is a trait that leaders in the 21st century are going to have to strengthen. Adapting to the rapid pace of change—accepting advances in technology, having the ability to be nimble, to let go of the "We've always done it this way" mindset—will be necessary for any organization to thrive.

CULTIVATE A CONTINUOUS IMPROVEMENT MINDSET

Your team should always be focused on improving their skills, both personally and professionally. As a leader, you can help them by letting them make their own decisions and come to their own conclusions. You need to trust them enough to let them make mistakes and learn from them, then be willing to guide them to improve. I'm not suggesting you throw them to the wolves, but enable and empower them to make informed decisions. If they do make a mistake, show them how they can do better next time.

If you spend your time micromanaging everyone, then you don't have a team; you have a group of underlings who are just doing what they are told. While you don't want people to fall on their faces, if you've done your hiring and training properly and pro-vided helpful feedback to your employees during informal or formal reviews, they should feel confident in their roles.

Jon and I always had the mentality that we needed to put people in the right positions and grow them professionally. This approach is cost effective because it lowers turnover; more importantly, it promotes loyalty. We have a commitment to grow our people.

To do this, start by identifying the people who have are resilient, trustworthy, and dependable, and who have a commitment to continuous learning, authenticity, and transparency. When you see this potential, put them in a position where they can learn and grow into a leader. If you put the right people into the right positions, everyone wins.

A word of caution: just because someone is great at their job does not mean they are ready to be a leader. Some people are born worker bees. Promoting someone who is a good individual contributor into a position of leadership can backfire, especially if this is not their strength and they are not prepared.

As they work to improve, everyone is bound to make mistakes—leaders and employees alike. However, it's important to not let your ego get in the way. Admit mistakes early, pivot, and move on. Don't be hesitant to make the next decision because of a previous mistake. In today's changing business climate, you have to be agile. If you make a bad decision, acknowledge it and be transparent. No one is perfect. We grow from our mistakes if we are open to learning from them.

MAINTAIN YOUR REPUTATION

It's important to roll up your sleeves and pitch in. More than likely, you know how to do most everyone's job because you did it yourself when you launched your company. Your team should see that leadership is willing to help out in a crunch. This builds trustworthiness and credibility with your employees. Once your credibility is gone, it's almost impossible to recover. Your reputation as a leader is to be guarded at all times.

I learned this from my mother, who used to talk to me about my credit score. She would say, "All you are is your credit score. If you mess that up, it's really hard to fix." It's the same thing with your reputation. I'm grateful I learned that lesson at an early age.

Something else I've learned is that as a leader, you also have to pay attention to your gut. Listen to that angel on your shoulder who tells you something is a bad idea or to walk away from a situation. Think before you speak. Think about the consequences of your actions. Maintaining your reputation is all about the decisions you make and the actions you take on a daily basis. It's doing what you say you will do and keeping your promises.

My company is in the business of helping our clients keep their brand promises by providing them with outstanding facility management services. Our work enables them to maintain a great reputation with their employees and customers. We couldn't do that if we didn't walk the walk ourselves. Credibility breeds credibility. Trustworthiness breeds trustworthiness. To be an inspiring leader and to create future leaders, you have to lead by example.

 To learn more about leadership and its impact on company culture, check out the *#BeBetter with Michael Kurland* podcast "Leading with Creativity and Compassion Instills Trust" with Monica Kang, Founder and CEO of InnovatorsBox®. Go to MichaelKurland.co/BeBetter-Podcast.

CHAPTER 13

BE BETTER

Starting Today

When I drove from New York to California, becoming an industry thought leader, podcast host, or even writing this book were not on my immediate to-do list. My brain was circling around things like securing clients, finding good vendors to perform the services those clients would need, and of course, turning a profit. I was determined not to fail, and I put all of my energy into these tasks.

It wasn't until years later, at the recommendation of my public relations firm, that I joined the Young Entrepreneurs Council (YEC) to share my thoughts on topics like company culture, leadership, team building, and more. At first, I contributed to a Q&A panel, which quickly turned into writing articles that would be published on sites like Forbes.com, Inc.com, and others. Today, I am a regular contributor on the Forbes Business Council and have led workshops at industry association events.

I have also launched my podcast, *#BeBetter with Michael Kurland,* in which I talk to purpose-driven leaders who are examples of the Be Better commitment. These inspiring business owners, CEOs, and solopreneurs have shared their stories of overcoming challenges and stepping out of their comfort zones to pursue their dreams. Because of this, they have become outstanding leaders in their organizations and in their industries.

Before you decide to step out and share your expertise, whether it's by writing LinkedIn posts or launching a podcast, you need to identify your message. You don't just wake up one morning and decide, "I'm going to be a thought leader!" It takes time and patience to build a following and rise above the noise. Otherwise, you're just another voice in the crowd, and people will eventually tune you out, hurting both you and your company's brand.

You need to provide valuable content that you believe in and can speak to expertly, on whatever platform is best for you. No one is going to ask me to speak on the latest technological innovation or the impact of evolving accounting principles. They will call me to talk about my facility management industry expertise and purpose-driven leadership.

Getting those calls didn't come on day one of Branded Group— they didn't come on day 100 either. Building your personal brand is a process, and you have to be prepared to ramp up slowly. It doesn't happen immediately, and you may need a team of people to help you.

Think of your personal brand. What do you stand for? What do you aspire to be?

It's important for any business owner to identify their "why" for launching a business. If it's solely to make money, that's fine. Just own up to that and make it plain to your team. If it's to leave a legacy or become a thought leader, great. Whatever it is, it needs to be embraced and lived out in all that you do.

Remember, you're a CEO trying to build and grow a business. Your team depends on you to keep the business profitable. They didn't come to work to watch you become famous. They are working for you because they believe in your vision, and they want to experience their own personal and professional success.

What you do impacts your team, your clients, and your reputation. The decisions you make are hinged on what you deem is important, the vision for your business, and the vision for yourself. For me, company culture and being an authentic, purpose-driven leader are key. That's my sweet spot, whether I'm making a sale or hosting my podcast.

I've shared a lot of information about what it means to be a Be Better leader and how, because of this commitment, my business, my team, and even I have become successful. This is what has worked for me and my company. It may or may not work for yours. This is why I stress the importance of being authentic and being yourself. Don't be a copycat. You can't do exactly what someone else did and expect to get the same results. You're not that person. You can learn from them and cherry-pick the approaches or decisions that make sense for you and your business, but expecting the exact same results is unrealistic.

Be authentic. Be vulnerable. Be gentle when you're delivering hard messages. Be kind. Be willing to do the same jobs you're asking your team to do. Learn from your mistakes, and don't be afraid to make hard decisions.

In writing this book, I wanted to encourage, maybe even inspire, others who are thinking about starting their business to take a leap of faith. Know who you are as a person so this translates into the leadership of your company and ultimately, into a culture that attracts talent and clients.

In these pages, I've shared my personal journey. This is what's worked for me. Developing an award-winning culture is not easy. People think company culture is a walk in the park. It's not. If it's done wrong, it's even harder to correct. You can't just hire someone, do a few brainstorming sessions or team-building exercises, and magically have a great culture. That is not how that goes. You have to weave culture into your road map from day one, because it's easier to get to where you want to be when you know what you want to achieve.

Our Be Better culture has evolved as Branded Group has evolved. This is how it should be for any organization. You must always strive to be a better version of yourself every day.

Here's a recap of my 13 Ways Not to Fail at Life and Leadership:

1. Be Connected—Business is about relationships. To be successful, connect to someone new regularly, either virtually or in person.
2. Be Teachable—Always be willing to learn something new about your business, yourself, your team, or your community.
3. Be Fearless—Never be afraid to step out of your comfort zone. Take leaps of faith to move your business forward.

4. Be People-Centric—It takes a village to grow a business. A team of diversely talented people will ensure your success.

5. Be Future-Driven—When it's time to expand, have a solid team in place and be ready to support them.

6. Be Purposeful—Create value for your clients and your employees with your products and services. Align purpose and profit.

7. Be Engaging—Your team is your most valuable investment. Keep them engaged with ongoing training and opportunities for advancement.

8. Be Profitable—Keep an eye on your bottom line by establishing KPIs that accurately measure your business growth.

9. Be Service-Oriented—Solve your client's problems better than anyone else.

10. Be Efficient—Have a mindset of continuous improvement so processes and procedures add value to the customer experience.

11. Be Generous—Give back in whatever way you can to improve your community and the world. Leave it a better place.

12. Be Inspiring—Be a CEO who inspires others to push past fear, reject complacency, and Be Better every day.

13. Be Better—Business success does not happen overnight. You have to know what kind of company you want to launch and lead. You have to lead by example—authentically, vulnerably, and transparently.

To be a better leader, you simply have to Be Better.

To learn more about investing in and inspiring others, check out the *#BeBetter with Michael Kurland* podcast "An Act of Kindness Can Change Your Business and the World" with Joe Scaretta, co-CEO and Founder of CS Hudson. Go to MichaelKurland.co/BeBetter-Podcast.

ACKNOWLEDGMENTS

If you would've told me I was going to write a book when I set out to launch Branded Group nearly a decade ago, I would've said, "Never." However, if I have learned anything, it is to never say never. My success at Branded Group has only been achieved because of the extraordinary people I've had the privilege of calling friend, mentor, valued client, dedicated team member, Mom, Dad, and most recently, wife.

Branded Group's vision to Be Better was realized because of the unwavering support I received from these outstanding human beings. There are not enough words to express my gratitude and love for each of them.

To say I wouldn't be where I am today without my mom and dad is both literally and figuratively the truth! Mom—Thank you for being my mom, for putting up with me and all of my crazy antics growing up. I know you worried about me, but it's all good now. Dad—I wish you were here for me to tell you in person, but thank you for instilling a strong work ethic in me. You always said you didn't have to be the smartest guy in the room; you just had to work the hardest. Thank you both for believing in me.

My sister, Meredith—We sure had some fun times growing up! Thank you for always being there for me, for listening to all of my ranting, and for never judging me. I'm so proud of you and all of your success!

My former bosses, Michael Sadi and Moses Carrasco—Thank you for showing me the ropes of corporate America and how to navigate those ropes without getting burned. You taught me valuable lessons on how to sell myself, how to deal with different types of personalities, and how to rise above the noise.

Joe Scaretta—Thank you for sparking a fire in me, for showing me how to take client sales to the next level, and for showing me how to be competitive yet compassionate.

Bill Pegnato, my mentor, my friend—You took a fellow East Coast guy under your wing and answered every new business owner question with grace, wisdom, and understanding. You celebrated my successes and helped me navigate the bumps in the road. I'm grateful for our friendship.

Tarell Hannah, Faith Espinoza, Elena Boone, and Debbie Green, Branded Group's first clients—You gave us a shot when the ink on our business plan wasn't even dry. You believed in our vision to do facility management better and have been trusted and valued clients. I thank you.

Rob Satriano, my good friend—You have been a shoulder to

lean on (again and again) and have supported all of my ventures. Thank you for sticking with me through thick and thin.

Ric Franzi, Chris Schembra, Darin Hollingsworth—Being a guest on your podcasts was a privilege. Your enthusiasm and professionalism for your own shows rubbed off on me and gave me the confidence to host my own. I thoroughly enjoyed speaking with each of you about your Be Better journeys, as well as learning more about gratitude and how to strengthen our company culture. Thank you for helping me step outside of my comfort zone by ditching the scripted questions!

Taylor Martin, web designer extraordinaire—Your talent and ability to translate my vision into graphical representations for our amazing website, newsletters, and all things digital is spot-on every single time. Thank you for all you and your team do to make Branded Group stand out and differentiate ourselves in the industry!

Jennifer Bernheim, OnPurpose PR—A year or so after I launched Branded Group, I wanted to do a giveback program. I called you. That simple request transformed Branded Group. In addition to developing our award-winning One-for-One program, you worked with us to craft our vision, mission, purpose, and core values. Your passion for organizations to give back and to align purpose with profit has truly elevated our brand.

Jennifer Covello—You know my voice so well and have a unique ability to transform it into thoughtful communications. This book would not have been possible without your assistance. Thank you!

The Be Better Team, past and present—You are the heart and soul of Branded Group. Let's face it: without you, Branded Group would be just another facility management company. Your hard work through good times and bad, through all of the growing pains, and through a global pandemic has made us what we are today. I could not have done this without you. "Thank you" doesn't seem to be enough. I hope you know how much I care about each and every one of you.

Kiira Belonzi—Can you believe you agreed to trek cross-country and work out of a closet 24/7 to build Branded Group? Those early days were rough, but you stood by me. You believed we truly could Be Better, and I'm forever grateful to you for taking that risk. I know we fight like brother and sister, but I appreciate your insights and how you push me to think differently.

Jon Thomas—The man. The master of all things data. The inspiration to Be Better, from day one when you fixed our email system. Getting us ready to work remotely before anyone knew the term "pandemic" is a testament to your incredible intelligence. Thank you for taking on the burden of, well, everything so that I could pursue things like social impact programs, podcasts, and this book.

Alejandra, my amazing wife—You've been there through it all. It's been a roller-coaster ride and you have always had my back. I look forward to many years of happiness with you. I love you.

ABOUT THE AUTHOR

As the CEO of Branded Group, Inc., an award-winning facility maintenance company, Michael Kurland is committed to leading with purpose. His determination to Be Better was the driving force in the launch of his company and has led to its exponential growth, cultural transformation, innovative social impact programs, and cultivation of a highly-regarded team of industry experts.

With a diverse background in sales and marketing, Kurland's vision is to create a conscious business that inspires future humanitarian leaders. He lives in Huntington Beach with his wife, Alexandra, and their dog, Harvey.